The Other Side of Me

A Journey into the Mystical
&
the Gems Revealed

Manuel Jose Muros

Published by:
Manuel Jose Muros
Newburyport, MA 01950

Copyright © 2018 by Manuel Jose Muros. All rights reserved

Paperback - First edition 2018

All rights reserved. No part of this book may be used or reproduced in any manner without prior writtern permission from the author and publisher.

ISBN: 978-1-7326458-0-6

Dedication

I dedicate this book to the loving memory of "Mima", who embodied many of the teachings I share with you. I have been blessed to have her as my mother and teacher, and now as an angel in my life.

Also to my three sons: Christopher, Jonathan, and Nathaniel who fill my heart with pride, love and Joy.

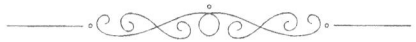

Contents

Acknowledgements

Introduction

PART I	Autobiography - A Journey into the Mystical

Chapter One   Paradise 5
Chapter Two   The Dark Times 9
Chapter Three   A New Beginning 15
Chapter Four   A Dream Fulfilled…or so I thought 19
Chapter Five   Time in the Pressure Cooker 25
Chapter Six   A New Dawning 31

PART II   The Gems Revealed 43

Introduction to the Teachings

1   Timeless Wisdom 48
2   Rest in Contentment 50
3   Heart Centered 52
4   Express Yourself 54
5   From Healing to Giving 56
6   Cultivating Presence 58
7   Moving Towards Silence 61
8   The Power of Our Words 63
9   The Colors We Carry 65
10 Every Day Starts as a Blank Slate 67
11 The Importance of Right Company 69
12 Life is an Inside Job 71
13 Co-Create Your Life 73
14 Experiencing Love 74
15 Quality vs Quantity 77
16 Creative Expression 78
17 Following Grace 81
18 The Light Within 83

19	A Reflecting Pond	84
20	Practice Leads to Transformation	86
21	Moment, to Moment, to Moment	88
22	Inner Harmony	90
23	Self-Love / Self-Acceptance	92
24	Fundamentals	94
25	Beyond Emotions	96
26	Free Will: The Human Experience	98
27	The Gate Keeper	100
28	It's Not What We Do, But How We Do It That Truly Matters	102
29	Yoga's Purpose & Power	104
30	The Enlightened Ego	106
31	Tending Our Garden	108
32	Love's Conduit	110
33	Keep It Simple - Keep It Positive	112
34	Be Your Authentic Self	114
35	The Gentle Whisper	116
36	Divine Timing	118
37	Inner Knowing	120
38	Dive Deep!	122
39	Our Unfolding Lives	124
40	Uniquely You	126
41	Love & Silence	128
42	Be an Empty Vessel	130
43	Dedication and Practice	132
44	Follow Your Passion	134
45	Being in Love	136
46	The Soul's Window	138
47	Listening	140
48	The Lost Art of Non-Doing	142
49	Liberation	144
50	Be Centered	146
51	Yoga is a State of Being	148
52	Emotions are Reflections of Attachments	150
53	Being Ordinary	152
54	It's Our Choice	154

55	Passing Through	156
56	There is Only One Answer	158
57	Creating Freedom	160
58	Navigating Life	162
59	Flowing with the Natural Cycles	164
60	Divine Guidance	166
61	God Consciousness	168
62	Magic Happens!	170
63	Let Spirit have its Way with You	172
64	Personal Revolution	174
65	Look Within	176
66	We Are It	178
67	Perfect Health is our Natural State	180
68	Situations Will Not Change Until You Change	182
69	Travel Light	184
70	Life, Our Lover	186
71	Becoming	188
72	The Fire of Transformation	190
73	Love is All There Is	192
74	Holding the Mirror	194
75	Follow the Rhythm	196
76	Thoughts and Karma	198
77	What Turns You On?	200
78	Live in Love & Joy!	202
79	Oneness Consciousness	204
80	Spiritual Bathing	206
81	What Are You Nourishing?	208
82	Stop Seeking	210
83	Grace	212
84	Make it Real	214
85	Illumination	216
86	The Oasis is Real	218
87	You Are Not Alone	220
88	Between Worlds	222
89	Our Creative Power	224
90	Master Creators	226
91	Find Yourself	228

#	Title	Page
92	Enjoy the Mystery	230
93	Our Bank Account	232
94	Loving Love	234
95	Living Without Fear	236
96	Inner Strength vs Outer Power	238
97	One Absolute Truth	240
98	Create From Within	242
99	The Path of Least Resistance	244
100	Feel Each Moment	246
101	Make Love with Life	248
102	Yoga is not Exercise	250
103	Nirvana	252
104	The Mystical Breath	254
105	God is All - All is God	256
106	Stop Seeking - Start Seeing	258
107	Inner Light	260
108	Just Plug In	262
109	I am Light… Experiencing Life	265
110	One Problem One Solution	266
111	Be Still… Listen	268
112	Bow	270
113	Draw into Your Center	272
114	Footprints	274
115	Yoga: Shift in Consciousness	276
116	Formless Form	278
117	Dream	280
118	Light Dancing in the World of Shadows	282
119	Traveling Through Life	284
120	Free-Fall Into God	286

Acknowledgments

To the great wisdom teachers that have lit the spiritual path for us to follow and explore. The great teachers and prophets, monks and yogis, artists and scholars that have dedicated their lives to understanding, knowing, and then sharing their wisdom and experiences.

To my many dear friends and fellow students of life that over the years have supported me on my path and who encouraged me to write down my experiences, thoughts, and words.

To my friend and fellow teacher, Nancy who shared her mastery of the English language to skillfully edit the book.

I am very grateful for the loving support and clear message of my sister and brother that I keep my energy focused on my passion and continue to bring these insights and teachings to life within myself and to give them light with my words.

To Mariella, the daughter I always wanted. She has accomplished the amazing job of creating and designing the cover and overall layout of the printed book and ebook. Her creative genius has brought beauty and order to my words.

I am most grateful for my amazing partner Alise, who, once she read some of my writings, took it upon herself to make this book a reality. With unconditional love and support, she has been the driving force in the complete process of publishing this book. She has become the wind beneath my wings that is inspiring this "contented monk" to share and engage with the broader world.

Acknowledgments

To the great wisdom teachers that have lit the spiritual path for us to follow and explore. The great teachers and prophets, monks and yogis, artists and scholars that have dedicated their lives to understanding, knowing, and then sharing their wisdom and experiences.

To my many dear friends and fellow students of life that over the years have supported me on my path and who encouraged me to write down my experiences, thoughts, and words.

To my friend and fellow teacher, Nancy who shared her mastery of the English language to skillfully edit the book.

I am very grateful for the loving support and clear message of my sister and brother that I keep my energy focused on my passion and continue to bring these insights and teachings to life within myself and to give them light with my words.

To Mariella, the daughter I always wanted. She has accomplished the amazing job of creating and designing the cover and overall layout of the printed book and ebook. Her creative genius has brought beauty and order to my words.

I am most grateful for my amazing partner Alise, who, once she read some of my writings, took it upon herself to make this book a reality. With unconditional love and support, she has been the driving force in the complete process of publishing this book. She has become the wind beneath my wings that is inspiring this "contented monk" to share and engage with the broader world.

Introduction

Over many years, my friends and students at The Yoga Center have been encouraging me to create a collection of the teachings I share. The discussions have always been fruitful, but there has been nothing tangible to take home. So I began recording and sharing some of the lessons as well as making an effort to capture the underlying message of my unique perspective on life.

My "awakening", combined with over twenty years of practice and dedication, have given me a perspective and direct experience of a spiritually grounded life that many find useful in navigating their own lives.

I maintain a daily practice of study, meditation, and contemplation, that comprises the majority of each day. I decided to start writing in this space of inner connection and the teachings began to flow. Many times a topic would come to mind and I would begin to write, finding a whole new perspective unfolding, leaving me surprised at what I had written. As you will see, some are straight forward teachings, others poetic, but they all point to an inner journey of "unknowing" to experience your True Self. Before you can go to unknowing, there comes an acceptance of who we are, as we are.

This book is divided into two parts: My autobiography, which details my early years through my mid forties, including the process by which life opened me up to the truth of my own being, followed by 120 contemplations on life and our spiritual journey.

PART I

Autobiography

My Journey Into The Mystical

1

Paradise

With no logical option I could see, totally beaten to my core, I walked into the empty church at the end of my street.

Defeated, I surrendered. I sat down in a pew and said to my God "I give up, I don't know what to do and I don't even care, just keep us safe…. All I really want is to know you. I don't want to know about you. I want to know you." ….. That was the beginning of my life becoming alive!

Twenty-five years later…

I write these words as I am completing the sixth decade of my current life and in full awareness that I am now beginning another chapter, one full of love, peace, and joy.

I've had a life generous of both blessings and hardships that have served to mold me into the person that I am today. I have chased dreams, experienced disappointments and heartaches, have loved and been loved. I have certainly had several distinct lives in just this lifetime. The outer world has taken many forms and yet there has been a consistent "me" that has been experiencing the journey.

Looking back I can see the perfection of life's journey. In times of hardship the right lessons are learned and in the good times we can see the love and the beauty. There have been stepping stones and signs to show the way and they have always been what I have needed, sometimes sour, sometimes sweet.

My journey began in La Habana, Cuba, where I was born on July 8th 1959. Fidel Castro had just taken power and was quickly disrupting the life as Cubans knew it. I entered into a privileged life of family farms, country clubs, beach houses, adoring parents, grandparents and extended family.

My life in Cuba felt like the Garden of Eden; horses to ride, rivers and beaches to swim, nannies, grannies, family, and friends all seemed to be there just to make my life perfect and beautiful. Always joyful and safe, simply paradise!

My family lived in a picture perfect small town in the center of the Island. It was where both my French and Spaniard grandfathers had settled after arriving from Europe and where both my parents were born. My paternal grandfather was a photographer and my maternal grandfather was a cattle rancher. My father was a very successful businessman who held the exclusive rights for Kodak products in Cuba, owned a furniture factory and continued to run the photography studio founded by my grandfather. My mother graduated from the University of La Habana as an educator but she was an artist in spirit.

Some of my happier memories were riding on my uncle's motorcycle with no helmet, sitting on the gas tank, held by his arms along my side. They were short rides to my grandfather's farm with a stunning river and waterfall that I remember riding the horses so deep that my legs would get wet. There was an old tree that nature had hollowed out creating a natural oven where we would roast pigs and have family gatherings along the river bank.

Then, when I was just seven years old, Paradise began to crumble. My maternal grandfather, Abuelo Rogelio, whom I adored, had a heart attack and died in my home. As everyone scrambled to get the local doctor, I sat alone next to him as his life slipped away. I thought he was going to sleep but he never woke up... That was the last time I saw him and the last time I was in my home. Unknown to me at the time, my parents where making plans to leave Cuba and my mother was too distraught to return home after the funeral. In one swoop I said goodbye to my world as I knew it.

On Sept 23rd 1967, as a young boy leaving my beloved homeland of Cuba for Madrid, our four propeller engine plane encountered a hurricane in the center of the Atlantic Ocean. Unable to withstand the force of the storm the pilot tried to fly above it to an altitude beyond the plane's capacity. The whole plane was vigorously shaking and oxygen masks were discharged as we started to lose oxygen and compression. The crew was praying and the passengers crying in the realization that we may not survive this flight toward freedom. The pilot sent "mayday" distress signals as we continued deep within the storm. We finally made it through to the other side but the plane was badly damaged. We had to make an emergency landing on the Azores Islands of Portugal.

We were devastated to leave our loved ones, our personal possessions, and the life we knew in Cuba, but through the Grace of God we got the opportunity to start a new life, as immigrants, in the land of my ancestors. Our time in Spain was short but in many ways extremely beautiful to me and there was this promise of a new dawn.

Unknown to me, a tremendous burden was placed on my older, dearest sister. The death of my grandfather and our exile from Cuba had severely challenged the mental and emotional health of my parents. They were overwhelmed by the immensity of it all and scared of the unknown future that awaited all of us. This was kept hidden from a very joyful eight year old boy.

My parents kept saying that we would soon be in the US, in the "promised land", full of beauty and opportunity. Somehow, they would tell my sister and me, "once we make it to our final destination things will be even more perfect than the life I knew and adored". Unfortunately, with great expectations there can be sad and devastating disappointments!

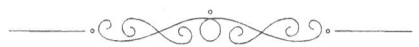

2

The Dark Times

In May of 1968 we arrived at NYC's John F. Kennedy International airport. We were greeted by my father's youngest brother Aldo who had been living in Union City, NJ. He was delighted to welcome us and to bring us to his home where his wife and his four children where waiting for us. There was relief in my parents faces to be with loving family. We took the long car ride through the Lincoln Tunnel, the longest I had ever experienced, to their humble apartment.

While my cousins and my aunt and uncle couldn't have been more loving and accommodating, they could not take away the overwhelming disappointment and disbelief of what was to become my new home, my new life. They lived in a two bedroom, one bath first floor apartment of a two family home. Used to the open space and bright lights of Cuba this place couldn't have been more claustrophobic and depressing!

The next morning my cousin took me out for a walk in the neighborhood. I simply had never seen a place that was uglier or more suffocating. Next to the house was an abandoned lot in disrepair and half a block away was the storage and repair station of the town's bus system. There was the constant pollution and noise of idle buses. Everything seemed grimy and dilapidated. This was my introduction to the United States and I did not like it at all.

An empty feeling of "paradise lost" remained with me through most of my adult life. Those early years showed me a harsh world of nasty, ignorant, and biased people. Fortunately the love and safety of my home never wavered and there was a place of refuge at the end of every day.

I started school without knowing the language and was placed in the regular fourth grade class; the school year ending in about a month. The teacher recommended that I pass to the next grade as my knowledge of science and math was adequate. She felt that I could soon learn English. This was a period of early migration of Cubans to this area. There were no other Cuban kids in my class and no one to connect and speak to during my school day.

There was such a disconnect between how other students and some teachers perceived me and who I knew myself to be. I grew up in a family of position and respect where everyone was kind, thoughtful, and refined.

The majority of these kids came from uneducated and rough families whose initial inclination and social conditioning was to pick and harass the new kid that was small in size and different from them. The teachers were a mixed bag, from kind and helpful to not really wanting to deal with a child that they could not fully communicate with. I felt a real sense of being unseen and stereotyped and not being recognized for who I actually was.

Thank God I had a fairly healthy sense of worth. It helped me to fight back physically, mentally, and emotionally; to reassert my identity in this new and challenging world. I quickly learned that bullies would back down if you took them on. In other words, I did not have to win the fight, they just needed to know that they were not going to get a free ride. They needed to know that I would inflict enough damage not to be worth the trouble. I also lost much of the fear. A few scrapes really did not hurt much and my ego would remain intact!

A certain armor and determination was cultivated during those early days of school. It was a bit of a jungle and you needed to know what you could handle on your own and when to get and ask for help.

The only time when things could have really gotten out of control was when this kid in middle school started to pick a fight with me during school hours. When school ended and I was walking home he came over with some friends and started to taunt me, pulled a jack knife out and started to swing it towards me. It was trash day and I was able to grab a metal trash can, placed it between us and started hitting him with it. He lost his balance, fell back and dropped the knife as I kept hitting him. When I let him get up he just ran away. That was the last physical fight I ever had. Something changed in me and I was no longer a potential target or victim in anyones eyes.

I grew up listening to the wisdom of the Cuban elders that surrounded me. Endless stories of their golden days and a poignant desire to recreate what had been lost.

Within a year of arriving, my father opened up a photography studio where I worked everyday after school and during weekends until I left for college. We would spend endless hours in the darkroom chatting about everything. Many gems of wisdom were shared with me; how education was the only thing no-one could take away from you, the importance of honesty and integrity, being your own person, family values, maintaining your independence, don't be a jack of all trades. Become the best at something you enjoy.

The dark side of these days is that my parents had entered survival mode and while there was plenty of love there was no time for play and joy. Life was a battlefield that you competed in for your survival. Only work mattered to my father to re-create a sense of security. There were no family vacations, social gatherings, sports, nor any "unnecessary indulgences". They had been dance champions at the local country club in Cuba and I never saw them dance again.

At the age of fourteen, my sister brought home a potential suitor, a Cuban boy her age who's family emigrated when he was three years old. Pete was blond, tall, a jock and totally comfortable in his environment. They fell in love, I acquired an older brother and they are still happily together, four kids and eight grandkids later!

Pete was instrumental in showing us that there was a bright future out there within our reach. It would take time and effort but it was there for our taking. Pete took me under his wing and has been the best brother I could have asked for.

One day we went to visit one of his high school buddies. He lived in a very modest apartment and there was nothing special I could see in him. Bob was explaining to Pete how one day he was going to run for president. He figured that there was going to be a big influx of Latinos into the US and he was born here but of Cuban parents, making him eligible to run and be a new type of leader. This was around 1969 and he had a detailed plan.

I remember thinking this guy is delusional, there is no road from here to there, yet I can still hear his words. They made an impact on me! Well this guy is Robert Menendez, the Senior US Senator from the State of New Jersey. I don't think he will be running for President but he is in the most exclusive club of our Nation.

While I was still in elementary school we lived in a rented apartment of a three story brick building. The downstairs had a retail space and there were two apartments on top. We lived on the second floor and my father's best friend from Cuba had just moved into the third floor unit. This building was on the same block as our photography studio.

One weekend night as my parents and sister were asleep I stayed up watching tv in my bedroom much later than I was allowed. When I turned the tv off to go to sleep I started to hear strange sounds in the stairwell: as if people were running up and down the stairs and then the crackling of wood. I thought someone was trying to break into our apartment. I got up and started calling for my parents.

When they rushed over to me and went to the living room, there was a massive fire burning through our front door which cut us off from the emergency fire stairs on the other side of the apartment. We dropped to the floor and crawled back to the front of the building which had metal bars on the windows. We called the fire department and my dad punched and kicked the bars off. Once the firemen arrived they carried us out through the window. My father's best friend and his wife were able to leave through the fire escape and when he did not see us come out from the back he went back into our burning apartment screaming for us, not knowing that we had gone out the front.

Someone had poured gasoline in the stairwell and set the whole building on fire knowing that there were two families living/sleeping there. Apparently the landlord had had a dispute with the retail tenant and evicted him and this was his way of getting back at him.

Within a few years, once again all of our personal possessions were lost. The building was demolished and the feeling of danger and uncertainty was all around me.

There was a silver lining out of all of this. The older lady who owned a block of buildings including the one housing my father's studio offered to sell him that building so we could have our home upstairs. She decided she did not want to deal with things as they were and put the other buildings up for sale soon afterwards. My uncle was able to buy one and he opened his general medicine practice there. The family had begun to create roots.

When I was sixteen I met my childhood sweetheart, Mariana, someone I could envision a life with and who would be my partner in creating a life far away from Union City. Both her parents were Cuban but she had been born in NYC. She was spunky, wise and full of life.

Mariana's mother was very old country and rigid with her. We needed a chaperone to go out anywhere and she made our young lives difficult. I was accepted to Mass College of Pharmacy in Boston but her mother would not let Mariana go away to a college.

I started college a year before Mariana. Her mother would not let her apply to a school in Boston. We both knew we wanted to be together so we proposed to both of our parents that we wanted to get married and continue with our education but would need their blessings and support. Mariana was seventeen and I was eighteen (one week shy of nineteen) when we got married and I actually became Mariana's legal guardian.

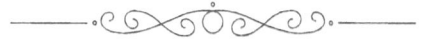

3

A New Beginning

Boston was a whole new world full of opportunities and challenges. We really found our stride with friends and school and started to carve out a place for ourselves. We were the only married couple at our undergraduate schools and our apartments became a hub for our friends.

The 1st year of marriage we shared an apartment with my sister and brother as they were on the last year of medical school at Boston University. Upon their graduation we moved to a smaller apartment in Brighton.

There is more to this story… Mariana on her own had found a one bedroom apartment in a large building complex. When we arrived at the building, I realized it was the same building my brother and I had gone to see a year before and had never gone inside because I had had a bad feeling about it and so decided to keep looking. I had the same feeling again and for a second time refused to see it.

It was a very good deal and I had no logical reason not to see it. Mariana convinced me to go back and look at it. Against my intuition we took it. We lived in this unit for a month and both ended up minimizing our time there as it felt really creepy and uncomfortable but for no apparent reason. The building manager was a great guy that seemed to have taken a liking to us and when a unit opened up on the top floor he offered it to us at the same rent… This apartment was two stories with a large deck and quite beautiful, so we jumped on it and moved into it that same evening.

A couple of weeks later we drove down to New Jersey to visit family and when we came back the whole building complex had burned down. It was arson and once again all of our possessions were destroyed. I was twenty years old and this was the third time that I was "invited" to let it all go and move on with life. A great lesson in learning to follow one's illogical intuition!

Nonetheless, as victims of this fire we found a beautiful low income apartment on the Charles Rives in Cambridge a few blocks from Harvard Square. The fire had been all over the news and I did not even know then that the city had low income apartments. As students we qualified and were placed on top of the list due to our homeless situation. We were Divinely guided…Out of a challenge, came a real blessing in disguise!

The next few years were all about school and creating an abundant life. While in college, one of my best friends Ruben and I decided to start a side business. Ruben was part of one of the wealthiest families in Puerto Rico. His uncle had a nursery on the island and he asked us to distribute/sell his tropical plants in the Boston area.

In a few months we pre-sold containers of plants to the flower exchange and to the Market Basket Supermarket chain with a huge profit for us. At twenty-one years old we had pre-sold enough plants that we would earn a profit of over $100,000 each over the next year. That was a lot more money than any of our professors were making! It made me wonder what I was doing in school!

To see an opportunity and to create a path toward manifestation was very exciting. It gave me the personal taste of entrepreneurship that was part of my heritage. A sense of freedom I have carried for my whole life.

Unfortunately, there was no contract with Ruben's uncle. It was all done with good will on our part. With all the orders on hand Ruben's uncle sold the farm for a great profit for himself to a larger operation and Ruben and I never saw a penny for our efforts. For the first time, I directly experienced a very wealthy man with no remorse in taking advantage of others, including his own nephew. It was just part of doing business! No ethics, no morals…

Upon graduation from college Mariana and I both landed our ideal jobs. Mariana, at the State House as an aide in the Governors office and I, as Assistant to the VP of International Operations at Orion Research. Our professional careers had begun and soon after we both enrolled in Master's programs. A year later we bought our first home, a beautiful condominium in the Brighton/Allston line. It cost $55,000 with a $5,000 down payment.

We were busy creating an identity that was outwardly successful and that would take us to manifesting the "American Dream". We worked long hours and changed jobs. I completed my MBA and Mariana, her MA.

After a couple of years working for the State of Massachusetts at the Department of Mental Health and Retardation, the Deputy Commissioner had taken a liking to me and offered to mentor me in my career. He asked what would be my ideal job within the state and told me he would help me move in that direction.

Upon reflection I told him "I don't even want your job, not sure what I am doing here, other than to get a paycheck". After laughing at my candor he then asked "so what would you rather be doing?" … after a pause I knew that what I wanted was to be my own boss, be on my own running a successful business. He suggested that I look at what services the government contracted out and to become a vendor for the Commonwealth.

Within a year's time I had left my job with the state, incorporated a transportation company, through competitive state bids, landed a $660,000 contract, acquired financing, leased 12 vehicles and hired

20+ employees. Soon after, I picked up several smaller contracts which increased the revenue to over 1 million a year.

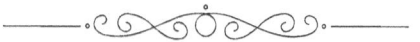

4

A Dream Fulfilled… or so I thought

Mariana and I started thinking about having a family and moving to the suburbs and we fell in love with Newburyport, a small historical city on the ocean and the Merrimack river north of Boston.

We found a beautiful 1840 Grand Greek Revival Colonial home with 14 rooms, 8 fireplaces and 5,000 square feet of living space….Just the right size for a young couple looking to start a family!.. Having been told we qualified to carry both mortgages and afraid we would lose this opportunity, we chose to do the bridge loan to purchase the new home as we sold the condo. It took us six months to sell the condo. It was nerve-wracking carrying all that debt. It was a great lesson that just because you can do something, doesn't mean you should!

Our $5,000 real estate investment turned into a $100,000 profit and our new company immediately started to produce a substantial income. There was a sense of having the "Midas touch" where everything we did would turn to gold. I was twenty-six years old and feeling on top of the world.

We completely rehabbed this old home and on August 14th 1987 beautiful Christopher Roger was born. I had become a father which felt both amazing and overwhelming! And less than three years later on April 9th, 1991 our precious second son Jonathan Louis was born. Life was full as we juggled work, kids and all of the demands of our modern society.

Approximately three years after moving to Newburyport, bank interest rates had started to drop and we decided to refinance our home with the local bank. As we were completing the process I saw in the local paper that the bank had foreclosed on the "Biddle Estate". A 1910 seventeen room, 10,000 square foot English Country Manor House on 4.75 acres of land with the Merrimack River in the front and the Pow Wow River in the back of the property. It was a like a fairy tale!

I called the bank president and asked if I could go to see it. He gave me the keys and said "we just approved your loan and worked out your finances. If you want to take over the bank note the house is yours and we will give you a bridge loan until you sell your current home".

The note on this home was very close to what we owed on our current house, it was basically switching homes as far as the mortgage was concerned but this old grand home needed some TLC and the cost of living there would be much greater.

Having had the past experience of a bridge loan we decided we would not do that as we were also quite happy with our current home. Instead we put our house on the market in the hope that if we sold it quickly enough we would then purchase the bigger home. Within a few months it all came together and by my thirty-second birthday we were moving into our "Estate" with our boys, a three year old and a five month old baby.

I had no idea what an impact this home would have on our lives. For us it was a grand old place to raise our boys, yet it unsettled many of our friends and colleagues. To the townies, this young foreigner was living in their grandest home.

The house came with quite a history. It was built by the largest carriage maker of that era, where Henry Ford and other industrialists of that time had come to stay. Built in a historical section with homes dating back to the 1600's… Biddle combined six properties to create his estate and had his own craftsmen build the home with all the intricate details you can imagine; leaded glass windows and book cases, silver and crystal hardware, mahogany woodwork and seven fireplaces.

The boys would ride their bikes inside the house. There was a hill that they sled down after winter storms and a tree house in the woods. We had started to create a life for the boys similar to what I had had in Cuba.

The transportation business was full of headaches and liabilities. With 20 + vehicles and 30 + employees there were too many moving parts all around Boston. Accidents, repairs, tickets began to drive our costs up and the state began to cut back on its programs. The future did not look very promising so I started exploring other business opportunities.

An entrepreneur is really an educated gambler, but non-the-less, still a gambler. Especially when you are starting out everything you own is being used as collateral for your next move, your next hand.

My brother and I had been admiring an extremely busy and well run hand car wash in Coral Gables, Florida, something that did not exist in the Boston area. We decided to join forces and he and my sister would help fund the new venture.

I quickly came across a new real estate development that was in the planning stages on Massachusetts Avenue in Arlington, right on the Cambridge line. It was an automotive dealership that had closed and would have three potential businesses on it: A CVS pharmacy and a McDonalds restaurant were planned for the front parcels and there was a great 12,000 square foot building that had been the repair bays in the back.

The developer and I immediately hit it off and came to terms as it was a perfect fit for all of us. As the project went through the town's planning board we started designing the building, looking at the equipment we needed to purchase and getting ready for a quick build out once we got the go ahead.

A non-profit vendor that had a transportation division became interested in taking over the transportation company around the same time. The state was amiable to extending the contracts and letting me transfer them over as it was a well run outfit. It was a blessing to be able to release the ever growing liabilities and leave with a reasonably good profit to carry us over for a few months until the new venture got started.

It all looked so promising, we kept hitting home runs in the game of life! New Jersey felt like a distant past and all I could see was sunny days in the horizon. The last thing I expected was the perfect storm that was to come.

We came to terms and sold the transportation company and focused our energies on the new venture. While we had quite a bit of equity, like most Americans we were living close to our cash flow and now the clock was ticking.

All of a sudden the project started hitting delays as the Arlington neighbors began to organize against having a McDonalds in their town. Public relations operatives got to work and the planning board meeting, postponed. I was promised it would all work out, but time kept passing and we had to start tapping into the money for the new venture just to keep our substantial personal expenses going.

Months into the project McDonalds recognized that they might lose and chose to pull out to control the damage to their corporate image. The developer, Bill, was able to quickly get another tenant on board and it appeared we were once again on track when I received a call from him. The planning director told Bill that even though by right we could place a car wash there, they did not want that in the town either and the whole development would be rejected. We would probably win an appeal but it would require carrying the property costs for two years and neither of us could afford to do that. While it was illegal and unethical, the town used delaying tactics and ultimately blocked us from creating our business.

What were we to do? With no income nor easy job prospects that could match our expenses we looked to see what else we could do with that building. How could we turn lemons into lemonade? … There was a new chain of indoor playgrounds called "Discovery Zone" that were an instant hit around the country. It was a chain created by the founder of Blockbuster Video and all the financial write ups were excellent. Our building would be a great location for it, so we decided to copy the concept and create "Fun in Motion".

5

Time in the Pressure Cooker

My life had become a pressure cooker as we were quickly eating up all the investment money that my brother and sister had set aside and nothing to show for it. We had to start from scratch with architectural and building designs for this new business, go after new financing, learn a new industry and go from concept to creation and operations. On top of that it was a business that I did not care for at all. It just needed to be done!

Along the way my brother and sister could not continue to put more money into the business and had to pull out. I had secured a business loan but needed more investment to close the deal. I went looking for potential investors as bankruptcy seemed to be around the corner.

At the last possible moment, Dick, a large real estate developer decided to become my 50/50 partner. He had the cash to complete the project and thought it would be a good industry to start investing in. Two days before losing the whole deal Dick and I came to an agreement.

To the outer world I looked like the definition of success. Beautiful wife, lovely kids, a red Jaguar and a white Land Cruiser, but inside I felt embarrassed for the financial loss I caused my brother and sister. Even if it was out of my control they still invested in me and my abilities and I had failed them. All this outer success simply felt empty, heavy, overwhelming.

On September 2nd 1994 our third son Nathaniel Joseph was born. We were blessed with another healthy and beautiful son. In the midst of all of our challenges this sweet soul came into our lives. Our home was filled with peace, love, and joy with our three boys and yet the outer world felt like a battle field that one had to enter daily.

Dick was worth over 100 million dollars in real estate. He was generating about 10 million dollars per year that he was looking to invest in new projects. As we were building out our new business we spent quite a bit of time together and I got to observe him and his operations.

He was self made having started as a handy man and taking quite a number of large gambles. He made it big with office buildings around Route 128. He was about thirty years older than me, seemed to enjoy our conversations and was clearly looking to have me be part of his world beyond this one investment. The opportunities seemed endless!

While Dick was always a gentleman with me I did see his ruthless side with his business dealings. He had a lawyer on staff that was always "battling" with contractors. On several occasions I saw him cut an excellent deal for a project, give the contractor a third of the money upfront and promised that this could lead to more business. Once the project was completed he would find fault where there really was none, delaying payments for months until the contractor was really hurting, and then settle for almost nothing.

He also shared battle stories of different ventures that had gone badly and how he got his money back from those that had none to be had. He saw nothing wrong with destroying people's lives. It was just business to him and it was very ugly and wrong in my mind. Even though he had all this wealth he was still behaving like he needed to scrape scraps off the table. The greed and lack of empathy was astounding and gave me a very bad taste for how many people behave in the business world.

In contrast, when my father returned to visit our hometown in Cuba, a man came looking for him. He wanted to thank him and offered to assist his visit in Cuba as he was now influential in the Government. He told him that he used to work for our furniture factory and at one point his mother had become very ill. My father found out about it, instructed the General Manager to send him home to take care of his mother and directed the Doctor and the Pharmacist to send him the bill for her care. My father simply said "that was just what one does when one can help someone in need".

The design and buildout of Fun In Motion turned out beautifully. We hired some great employees, invested heavily in promoting the business, and each section was running well as we got started. But, we were still not getting the numbers we needed. We kept working to control costs and increase revenue, but the formula was just not working.

We then found out that Discovery Zone was accused of "cooking their books" and that the stores had good starts but then fizzled out and the whole chain ended up filing for bankruptcy.

For months Dick kept investing more money to keep the business afloat as we waited for profits to arrive but they never did. We had no choice but to shut down. Dick found a new tenant which took care of our lease obligations and I sold the equipment and used that money to close the business down.

Dick and I were 50/50 partners which meant that one shares equally in the profits as well as the loss. Over a million dollars was sunk into this project! ... My whole world was crumbling all around me and I could not see a way out.

The greater the outer pressure the more I deepened into my faith. My mother and my maternal grandfather had deep spiritual roots that let them face personal challenges with peace and conviction. I kept praying for guidance, looking for a miracle that would somehow protect us from this storm... Then something amazing happened!

With no logical option I could see and totally beaten to my core I walked into the empty church at the end of my street. I surrendered. I sat down in a pew and said to my God "I give up, I don't know what to do and I don't even care, just keep us safe… All I really want is to know you. I don't want to know about you. I want to know you." … That was the beginning of my life becoming alive!

Sitting on that pew, a deep peace began to arrive. I felt embraced by this bubble of inner calm. I felt an unconditional love… I felt safe… Somehow we would be ok.

A window into the Divine had opened in me and I began to spend more and more time sitting in stillness drinking from this fountain, nurturing my soul. The external world was just as demanding and threatening but an inner peace began to take root in me. I felt like I was on a sail boat in the middle of a gigantic, nasty storm and all I could do was stay calm and weather out the storm… It was a very long and difficult storm bringing new challenges with every turn but my peace and stillness kept getting deeper and stronger. My connection to the Divine became the center of my life and my only real focus.

As I understand it now, my kundalini energy opened in my love for God and my surrendered state in the church pew. I began to "see" the world quite differently. I began to see energy fields and (except for the little kids) everyone looked like "zombies' absorbed in the stories of their own mind, not seeing what was really there in the present moment, but simply projecting their past and expectations into what was actually occurring.

I spent approximately two and a half years devotionally studying and meditating from twelve to eighteen hours per day seven days a week… I was in a "natural high" exploring this new world full of love and peace and contentment… God had revealed himself to me… He was in everyone and in everything… He is the love and the foundation of all Creation… He had answered my prayer!

Mariana called her old boss from the Governors office and explained our situation and asked if he had any leads for a job. She had left her work with an excellent reputation and within a week she was offered a temporary job until a more permanent position was available. A few months later that position came to be and she quickly moved up within the organization. With an income stream, we were able to subdivide and sell some property to cover our debt and to stabilize our situation.

God's grace kept showing us the way and created a path that kept our family safe without filing for bankruptcy. Mariana's career took over and she became the financial provider for the family, as I stayed home taking care of the three boys and fully devoting myself to my spiritual practices.

My "awakening" was extremely challenging to Mariana. Medically I could have been diagnosed as having a nervous breakdown, but I was actually in this place of deep peace and just not able nor willing to return to the life I had had. I had been transformed, but still not sure who I was becoming. She felt "abandoned" in that I no longer wished to continue in the struggle for external success. We were in two different realities.

One night after a very deep and extended mediation I had one of my most mystical experiences where I felt a total oneness with God and all there was. I knew that my soul could have just stayed there as this was our true home, our highest Self… I also realized that life was a gift and that I should continue with my journey. It was not time to go home as I had this whole life ahead of me. In my prayers I expressed that I would continue with my life but it had to be completely different. I was not returning to the fear, struggle, and sense of separation that had been my past experience.

I went to bed around 4am. Mariana later told me that when I laid down next to her, she was frightened as she felt as if a stranger had gotten into bed with her. My energy/vibration had shifted and her being recognized that change. She was losing her life companion to-something she really could not comprehend.

We spent several more years living under the same roof, raising our boys but our relationship changed to being more like siblings than a marriage. Few women would have had the strength and love to support their spouse under these difficult circumstances but Mariana did it with grace and love looking to do what would be best for our boys. I felt she kept waiting for the old me to return, but that "me" no longer existed.

A new life had begun in partnership with God. I was having daily experiences that my religion could not explain and I was guided to the ancient yogic teachings of consciousness. Enlightened masters had written about the path toward personal connection with our Divine self. They explained what I had experienced and helped make sense of my new reality.

During these many years, I have met with many psychics and gifted teachers who have affirmed my own experience and assisted me on my path to living a life from this higher perspective.

Many great prophets, saints, and teachers have shone a light for us to follow and I hope that with my words and teachings I can also add my light for those on this journey of life.

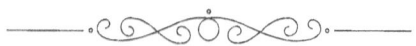

6

A New Dawning

So what do you do after you become "awakened"?

At first, life does not get any easier! As a matter of fact, there is a whole lot of new information to digest and figure out and unfortunately, there is much disinformation and half truths presented out there. Fortunately, we are never alone and there is much Divine guidance leading us along our path.

With this shift of vibration all relationships must adjust as you are in a new reality. It can be very challenging for everyone as basically all contracts are broken or renegotiated. New people start showing up and others leave as your work together is completed.

Your sense of reality cracks when you have "awakened" and now your ego needs to be reconstructed with this expanded sense of Self. Basically the veil is lifted for you, but you must still function in a world that remains veiled.

Normally your rational ego mind is doing all the driving and now you must learn to surrender to this new reality with no instructions. Only through experiences do you learn to navigate this new way of being that encompasses all of who you are. In a very real sense there is a refinement of your ego that allows it to open to the love and peace that dwells within.

Life is your teacher! In my case it brought the most interesting people and fascinating experiences to keep assuring me that I was not crazy and to stay steady on my path.

One of my early companions was Bea, an eccentric and quite stunning older lady who was very proud of being the first person in Newburyport to get a business license as a psychic. She used to lead the local Course in Miracles group and immediately noticed the "light" in me. She kindly spent many hours guiding me.

Once, at her home, we were meditating with our eyes open and I said to Bea "the room seems to be flickering as if it was pulsing in and out of reality". She began with this deep belly laugh and said, " I've been watching you appear and disappear for the past twenty minutes… hahaha" …

About a year after getting to know her, she informed me that she was moving to Mexico and that Spirit had instructed her that I was the one to continue leading her Course in Miracle Group that I actually had never attended! It was the first formal spiritual group that I led and it helped turn my home into a gathering place for like minded individuals.

The second person who was a stable constant at that time was Elayne. She was the Montessori preschool teacher of my two younger sons and a very talented astrologer and psychic, who for many years kept assuring me that this was my path and to trust the Divine guidance.

Around this time I also met Doug, ten years my senior and quite a character. Doug was brilliant, an alcoholic who had been sober since his twenties with anger issues, yet a total sweetheart behind his tough exterior. He was a true seeker and kept introducing me to many of the early teachers and healers that assisted me along the way.

Doug told me that there was an Australian mystic and teacher visiting in Kittery, Maine by the name of Leonard and would I accompany him to go to see him. He had written several books and had quite a following in Europe and Australia. His teachings were similar to Ekhart Tolle and "The Power of Now" but before his time.

Leonard was a bit aloof and distant with most of the folks at the gathering, but he made a point to connect with me and we made arrangements for the two of us to have breakfast the following week at the local diner. There was an acknowledgment of a shared journey.

At breakfast he shared with me that he was an attorney who had a near death experience drowning in the ocean. He experienced his spirit leaving his body and then coming back as he was resuscitated. This provoked his awakening and pursuit of cultivating the awareness of the present moment. I shared my story and my strong Christian faith that awakened me during my difficult times.

He was an atheist and totally challenged me to move beyond my religious faith to a more expansive view of the Divine. I hosted a gathering for Leonard at my home and we spent several days exploring our perspectives. He invited me to acknowledge the path that had taken me to this new awareness. He pushed me to get off that path and explore this new reality with fresh eyes, or I would not get the full benefit of what I was given. I found his advice to be true.

My next big expansion was when I met Steve Rother. Once again, Doug invited me to a weekend workshop in Southern Massachusetts. I had no idea what it was about. I was just happy to accompany Doug. He actually did not know anyone going but was interested in checking it out. I later found out that Steve was the first person to be asked to do a "Live Spirit Channel" at the United Nations and had a worldwide following. For the previous five years he came annually to this community from his home in Los Angeles. There were always forty-four people who attended. He did not control the number, it just happened that way and this was to be his last year.

We arrived and registered and as I started walking into the hall a man gently walked over to me and gave me a hug, and whispered in my ear "thank you for staying, we need you here" …. Energy moved right through my body and I started sobbing from deep within me. It was Steve. How did he know about my conversation with the Divine? He sees me for who I am!!! It was just overwhelming. Steve had not even seen my name, on the registration list, nor did I know anyone there other than Doug.

As I walked into the room looking to compose myself, this very sweet older lady came over to me, held my hands as she looked into my eyes and repeated the same exact words as Steve "thank you for staying, we need you here" and then she continued. "Don't worry, you are with family, you are safe, you are guided".

The whole weekend was just magical and for the first time I felt that I had a group of peers and a place where I was understood and seen as I saw myself. Back home most people did not know what to make of me as I had pulled out of the life I had been living, spending the bulk of my time in solitude and deep meditation.

There was much healing that needed to take place within me. Even though a window had opened into the Divine, my old wounds and unhealthy patterns would take time to be healed and transformed. There was much inner work to be done…

I was living in two separate realities. Deep in meditation I felt whole, complete, safe. In life I felt ungrounded, unsafe, and nothing really interested me. Everything seemed so unimportant compared to the utopia I could find within myself. I did what needed to be done but every free minute I would spend studying or meditating.

Doug was a good friend of Cate, the owner and founder of The Yoga Center of Newburyport. He invited me to attend some classes. Kate was a ball of energy, loud, brash, and a wild spirit. As we were doing the Asana (physical practice) Cate kept saying this was the path to enlightenment and I kept saying to myself "bull-shit, this is lots of work and has nothing to do with what I experience". Yet, I kept going back because it made me feel really good. Slowly the practice started to get me in touch with my body, a place I had pretty much left behind! I started to get grounded.

Soon I was taking classes seven days a week, sometimes two classes in a day exploring this new experience of me. Until one day Cate asked if I wanted to start teaching as my physical practice had surpassed her own and I was obviously committed to the practice. The teaching came easily and it really helped ground me even further. I was barefoot, leading a group of students in a physical practice that required intense focus and had a meditative component to it.... It was perfect for me! .... I had found a place from which I could engage with life.

One day after class, as I was sitting on the floor leaning against the wall I said to Cate "If you ever decide to sell the Center I'll buy it. What the hell, I am always here and there is no other place I would rather be"... She was happy running the Center and had no intention of selling it, but life began to take some interesting turns for her and within a year I bought the Center with my good friend Leigh.

The Center continues to be a sanctuary for myself and like minded folks. A truly spiritual community that uses yogic tools and teachings as a foundation toward mindful evolution. Over the years we have hosted the most authentic yoga teachers and scholars that we were pulled to study with.

In the early years of my awakening I kept looking for the "next high", the next experience that would "prove" to me that I was spirit and not just this body and personality. I continued to push myself with long hours of meditation and breath work as a way to increase the energy moving through my body. The physical practice helped anchor me and kept me grounded.

I decided to do a fire walk in our backyard and asked a friend, Dan, to lead it as he had years of experience. About a dozen friends came together to make the ceremony of a large bonfire and then walk on the burning coals as the evening set in. My oldest son Chris who was about eight at that time asked if he could walk with us and before I could answer his mother called out, "no way, we could not take the risk of him burning his feet and that was non-negotiable" … so I told Chris "you heard your mother but non-the-less you can be with us and stand next to me through the whole ceremony" .

Hours later after the coals had been racked and Dan was getting ready to do the first walk, I looked down at Chris and saw that he was playing with the coals with his barefoot. I looked around for Mariana and she had gone inside so I told Chris "do you still want to walk on fire?… walk next to me." We went in front of the line, breathed deep into the present moment and slowly walked across the burning coals.

Our feet were perfect and our spirits soared! This experience had a positive and profound impact on Chris. I must say that we were the only two not to have had some sort of "hot spot" on our feet. No one was badly burned but some did end up with small blisters.

For several years Mariana and I continued to live together, going on family vacations and maintaining a loving household for the kids, but emotionally we kept moving apart. At some point we realized that this really was not the most healthy example to give our sons as neither of us was truly happy living this way. Mariana and I were the perfect couple to our friends and family, having been together since our teenage years, but we needed to be honest with ourselves and give each other the freedom to find happiness in our lives.

The day after we filed our divorce papers, I headed off to India for a six week journey. My very good friend Mark and I planned on traveling for four weeks together and I would stay for an extra two weeks on my own.

Mother India is a truly special place full of contradictions and challenges. It is dirty and loud, full of poverty and ignorance and it is also the home to some of the greatest teachers and practitioners of spiritual practices that have lived on this planet. It is raw and alive, just what my soul needed at that time.

We flew into Bangalore and the next day took a bus to the Ashram of Ramana Maharashi where I found myself that evening eating on the floor from a large leaf that was used as a plate. No utensils, served by monks dressed with just a loin cloth, as monkeys played around in the courtyard. From the start it was so surreal and fantastic! I had entered a place that seemed outside of time, rustic and exotic in its natural state.

Ramana as a very young boy had gone to the local temple to ask the priest "who am I" and felt that no one could give him an accurate answer. So he went into a cave in the blue mountain and after several years moved to another cave in the same mountain and became a holy man meditating on that question. Many folks had gathered to be in his presence and over time built the Ashram that I was visiting right on the base of the mountain. I believe Ramana spent over twenty years in the caves before he came down mostly to serve his followers as it was too dangerous for them to be up in the caves.

The next day Mark and I hiked up the mountain. We meditated in the two caves used by Ramana giving me two very powerful experiences. In the first cave, I went in to what felt like hours of meditation and came out feeling badly that I had kept others from meditating there. But Mark informed me that I had only been inside for just a few minutes. I had entered a timeless place of deep peace and stillness, some sort of energy vortex that felt amazing.

We continued climbing to the second cave and once there sat for a meditation. When I walked out, I felt the earth shaking as if an earthquake was happening. I hugged the stone walls on the outside of the cave to stabilize myself as I thought I was going to fall down the side of the mountain. As I composed myself and looked around I noticed that the earth was not shaking, it was me who was shaking from the inside! I sat on the floor. It took a few minutes for my body to adjust and integrate whatever it was that occurred inside that cave. My trip to India had started in earnest. Within forty-eight hours I had experienced the power of mother India and Ramana would become one of the ascended masters that guides me still to this day.

After several days at the Ashram we hired a driver to take us to Pondicheri on the East Coast to the Ashram of Sri Auribindo, a contemporary of Ghandi. He was a scholar. The temple felt less open and accessible to us. We were unaware that it was the beginning of Monsoon season as it started to downpour.

The following day we headed to Auroville, an intentional community created by "the mother" who was Sri Auribindos' French partner. It was their vision to create a community that would embody the human potential. Within Auroville there is a modern temple, The Matrimandir.

We arrived in the rain and were taken to our chalet in the woods. That night the rain fell like buckets pouring and the frogs were making loud screeching noises that made my skin crawl. The grounds were getting flooded all around us. My back began to tighten up and I began to get very tense. The last thing I needed was for my back to go out at the beginning of our journey. In the middle of the night, I sat up and told Mark that in the morning I was heading back to our comfortable hotel in Pondichery and he could stay here if he wanted… Mark's reply back was "yes, you can do that if you want, now, just breath and relax" …. As I prayed and tried to relax I basically said to the Universe, if you want me to stay here the rain needs to stop. The energy was overwhelming to me. The next morning we got up to a mild drizzle and that remained for the week that we were there. As we departed the heavy rain returned.

We were able to get access to go inside The Matrimandir to meditate on two occasions. The first was in the 'outer petals' and the second, the inner chamber which has the worlds largest crystal at its center. In the first meditation I began to see all the loved ones in my life as they truly are: as spirit beings. I could feel their challenges and love in this lifetime. It was as if each soul came to let me see them as they really are. There was so much love and an incredible sense of our oneness. In the second meditation there was a profound sense of stillness and contentment. I received a vision of very young man that I did not recognize. Later as I was looking through one of Ramana's books I realized that it was him as a young boy.

Through a series of buses we made our way to the west coast by way of Bangalore and Mysore. For approximately a week we stayed with a local family in the largest Tibetan community outside of Tibet. It was fascinating to be with about ten thousand young monks that were studying in five large temples.

After a month of constant traveling we made it to Goa, where I planned to stay for the last two weeks on my own. Goa is known for the beach communities that are created for the fall and winter seasons and it is a place were many Europeans come on long holidays. I thought I was just going to relax but the Universe had other plans!

During our travels Mark and I kept an extensive daily yoga and meditation practice which in combination with so many new and exotic experiences helped us to deepen into the present moment, just savoring each day and the gifts that it brought.

I decided to take a yoga class on the beach that was being led by an Australian woman, Ann. We had a good connection. I found out that she was an energy healer, shiatsu practitioner, and a Reiki Master. She was not a very good yoga teacher nor practitioner and kept apologizing to me for her lack of abilities which did not really matter to me. This was a way for Ann to make money and to meet potential clients for her true gifts, her energy work. For over twenty years Ann had trained and worked in Japan with an energy healer, a real master.

My days were joyful with new friends I kept meeting on the beach, in yoga classes, at the local health food restaurant and during leisurely evenings at the beach clubs. I kept enough alone time for solid meditations and contemplation.

The Australian healer was offering a Reiki One training that some folks I had met were also attending, so I decided to join them. The training lasted a couple of days and it was very intense which made me interested in going deeper. Ann told me that it was necessary to wait a month before moving to the next level and apologized for not being able to share it with me, as I was leaving the following week.

The next day she found me and said that during her prayers the Reiki masters had told her that I could do the next level of energy work. Something she had not seen in her twenty years of experience. They instructed her to do a private with me. I joyfully agreed to do the session the following day.

When I arrived, she had been preparing herself and there was a deep stillness. We talked for a few minutes and she then instructed me to lay down. I closed my eyes in prayer and meditation as she went through her session. With my eyes closed I clearly saw two old Japanese men on either side of me taking part in the ritual. I could feel energy flowing through my body and all was peaceful. For some reason I began to move my fingers that I had over my belly and I felt completely ethereal as my fingers appeared to move through my belly. Once the session ended I stayed around for a while composing myself. I was wiped out!

The next morning I woke up and when I opened my eyes I could barely see. Both my ears were ringing and hurting. I had a double eye and double ear infection! In three days time I had to be back in Bangalore to catch my flight home and my body was a mess. There was a reason why this level of energy work was not done so intensely. I decided to take a cab to the local hospital for antibiotics to help the body recover. I had enough vision that I could get around but I did not want to get on a plane with achy ears. For the next few days everything felt surreal, somewhat out of time and space, slowly saying goodbye to India as my journey was coming to an end.

To get back to Bangalore I took a sleeper bus at 10pm and arrived early morning in the city. I headed to my hotel, meditated and slept for a good part of the day. I came out for an early dinner and a last walk through town, my ears still not fine. I kept praying for them to heal in time.

I arrived at the airport before 6am with my ears back to normal. I couldn't be happier, heading to Heathrow for my layover back to Boston. The terminal was fairly empty when I arrived. I sat and meditated as other passengers arrived. Soon most of the seats where taken. I walked around the terminal to stretch my legs and sat down next to a lady that had her eyes closed in what appeared to be peaceful contemplation. She had a book on her lap from Sri Baba.

After a few minutes she gently opened her eyes, looked at me and softly asked "who are you?" I did not really understand her question and said so, as I shared my name. In a very soft and loving way she said "truly, who are you? I could feel your energy even before you entered the terminal. I had my eyes closed as I was seeing Shiva dancing all around you".

We exchanged a little about ourselves. She lived in Belgium and had spent the last few weeks in Sri Baba's ashram in deep spiritual practice. She was fully open in the glow and high vibration of her experiences. We had been drawn to one another and became immersed in conversation.

We stood in line to board the plane and the passengers in front and behind us were pulled to the side by security to check their bags as we walked right by. As I sat in my window seat, I thought how nice it would be if the seat next to me remained free. It was a long flight to London but the plane was totally full. As we were ready to take off, I looked around and saw that the only free seat on the plane was the one next to me. With much gratitude I closed my eyes and continued with my prayers and meditation.

Often I have this feeling of floating through my life. I am here, but not really here. I am both having the experience as well as seeing myself having the experience. Being the seer and the seen. During my journey home this was quite magnified as I could perceive life opening to accommodate my path.

Heathrow was very busy. In line going to the other side of the air port for my flight home, security stopped our line for a few minutes and the person in front of me started complaining to the agent. Our eyes met as I was shaking my head in disbelief at the attitude of the passenger. As the agent let us pass he pulled me to the side and sent me to the priority line that was completely empty. I walked right through! Not that I was in any hurry, as my flight would not leave for a couple of hours.

The line at the gate began to form as we started to board. I was taking my sweet time as I had no hurry to get inside the plane and slowly joined the line. I looked toward the attendants doing the checking in and one of the ladies waved me over to the counter. There were probably twenty or so passengers in front of me. I gave her my boarding pass and she sent me through. Now I was really wondering what the hell was going on!!!

The flight was fairly empty and once again the seat next to me was not occupied. I had the window seat and there was a man on the aisle. He seemed to be a business man traveling with a couple of colleagues. Soon after takeoff he moved over to sit with one of his friends. I was left with the whole aisle to myself to lie down.

During my travels in India and on my journey home I was able to fully experience a different way of being on the planet. It solidified many of the experiences I had been having since my "awakening" in that church pew. I had a different relationship to reality. One that was full of peace, love, and some would say magic. I like to think of it as walking with "Grace".

PART II

THE GEMS REVEALED

Introduction To The Teachings

At some point you stop being the seeker and you start living, being in this new state of awareness.

The Buddha was asked, "What did you do before awakening?" His answer was, "chopped wood and carried water". He was then asked, "what do you do after being awakened?" and his answer was, "chop wood and carry water, but all is different".

We can only see and experience what our subconscious believes to be true. Our mind has filters from which we view life and those filters keep us in our narrow path of experience and awareness.

The path of awakening is commonly described as the transformation of a caterpillar into a butterfly with many analogies of the struggles that the caterpillar must go through in order to transform into that beautiful butterfly. There is also a time when the butterfly does not know its new qualities and must doubt its ability to fly.

We are accustomed to living with a sense of fear, lack, and separateness. Life is seen as a struggle that must be endured. Our transformation allows us to know that we are never alone. All we need in every moment is provided for us. Peace and silence within ourselves allows us to see the love and beauty that is ever present.

Every moment is full of realities and our awareness is what enables what we will perceive and experience. From lack to abundance, from fear to love.

There is a baseline of simple joy when one is contented with life's many gifts whether they are sweet or sour at any moment. Happiness is related to the outer world but Joy is cultivated within ourselves. The ability to see beauty and feel love rests in the eyes and essence of the beholder.

I live in the body of God and God experiences himself and his creations through me. We are one. He lives in me, I live in him…

Following are 120 teachings that I offer for your meditation and contemplation. These are concepts that I have explored and are the lenses from which I see life. Take them as starting points to explore your own inner world and to find your unique connection to the divine that dwells within you.

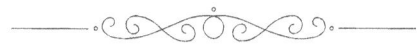

1

*Follow that inner wisdom, the life force,
that will always lead us to make the highest choice.*

Timeless Wisdom

It is very reassuring to read and connect to the deeper teachings through the different traditions and practices that span thousands of years and very diverse cultures.

There are fundamental teachings and practices that are followed by monks, knights, samurai warriors, yogis, saints, and shamans, all meant to transform from within and create a new higher way of engaging with life. These practices, slightly modified to align with the culture and the times, are meant to elevate us from the daily grind and place us in direct connection and service of a higher cause.

They may speak of being in service to "God, Allah, the Tao, Qi, Shiva/Shakti, the Four Winds, etc. They are all talking about aligning their lives to a higher force.

The Tao Te Ching, in its beautiful verses, describes how we should not lead our lives by external codes of conducts, instead we should follow that inner wisdom, the life force, that will always lead us to make the highest choice.

Notice that these seekers of truth are in service of others. They spend their time honing their practices, perfecting their movements, and connecting to deeper levels of stillness in their being. They don't do yoga or Tai Qi. They are Yogis, or Knights, or Samurai Warriors. They become embodiments of the highest teachings and beacons of light and hope for those around them. They inspire us and show us a well lit path.

Practice makes them masters of their thoughts and emotions. They become one with the perfection of the present moment. They learn and live by the wisdom of nature and their own hearts. They are humble in their ways because they are servants to a higher cause. They know that arrogance, self-interest, or non-truths would lead them astray from the force that sustains them.

Every time period needs its version of a knight, of a warrior. Our time period needs legions of light-workers. We all need to do our personal inner work to move from fear to love. We are all called to do our work of transformation in order to live in the peace and love acquired by a direct connection to the light within.

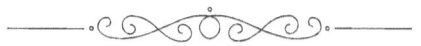

2

The real key to well being in all aspects of our lives is to learn to cultivate and then rest in contentment.

Rest in Contentment

Our mind loves to play tricks on us. It has this way of fooling us into believing that we cannot have quality in our lives until we accomplish a list of outer activities. We have a certain materialistic mindset that says once you have acquired things, then you will have this quality in your life. It is not really true.

Just a few examples for contemplation; 1. Once I have a partner, I will be happy and full of love. 2. Once I get that promotion I will be satisfied with my career. 3. Once I have saved x amount of dollars I will have abundance in my life.

The real key to well being in all aspects of your life is to learn to cultivate and then rest in contentment. Stop searching outside of yourself for the qualities that can only be developed internally. Once these traits live in you, they will bear fruit in your outer life.

Cultivating contentment allows us to deepen the experience we are actually having. We are able to settle and appreciate all the little things that create quality in our lives.

By not looking for the next best thing to make us happy, all this extra time and energy becomes available to enjoy what we already have. Levels of peace and well-being naturally arise.

I am not implying that you should not have things that you would like to do and see and experience and accomplish. In reality, all these things will flow much easier, if you are fully engaged and contented in each moment. Enjoy the journey as it takes you to your destination.

3

Our mind must bow to the wisdom of the heart and learn to follow its gentle guidance.

Heart Centered

To be centered in our heart is to be centered in the here and now. Instead of dredging up the past or projecting into the future, we "know" what is true in each moment.

The heart is able to feel, have empathy, compassion and unconditional love, which can shift any situation and brake us out of limiting patterns and beliefs.

As we cultivate silence in ourselves, we allow the wisdom of the heart to be heard. As we slow down our automatic reactions, we can respond with love and compassion.

Our mind's domain is logic and our heart is the compass that points to our true north. Our mind must bow to the wisdom of the heart and learn to follow its gentle guidance.

Joy, bliss, excitement and satisfaction can only be achieved by the guidance of the heart. It will take us to places we wouldn't dare enter and it will open us up to possibilities beyond our greatest expectations. But, it does demand that we let ourselves be guided by this inner wisdom that is illogical, as it operates from a whole other level of existence.

A safe life is lived under the fear and constraints of our mind but, in order to be fully alive we must follow the wisdom that dwells in our heart.

4

*This is only a game and nothing of value can be lost.
The true loss is not living your life to its potential.*

Express Yourself

When was the last time you danced? Sang? Had a belly laugh, and allowed joy and freedom to play you?

Surrender and become an instrument of God. Let his light sparkle through you, as you, and become the highest expression of yourself.

Don't take yourself too seriously, nothing is so important that you must give your light to it. This is only a game and nothing of value can be lost. The true loss is not living your life to its potential.

Only paper tigers are between you and your most magnificent self. Your self constructed fears and limitations are the only thing holding you back. The whole Universe lives within you ready to express itself through your dreams and desires.

Become one with your inner sun and all the shadows of lack and fear will disappear. Your authentic path will be brightly lit. Become your dreams, and from within roll out the life you were born to live.

Your outer world is but a reflection of your inner world. Release yourself from limiting thoughts and beliefs and allow God's light to lead your dance. Invite ecstasy and bliss to live inside of you. Surrender to the one true love of the Divine.

5

*When we are complete unto ourselves,
there is abundance in all aspects of our lives.*

From Healing to Giving

Our yogic path is a complete path that guides us back from fear, anxiety and ill health to a place of balance, love, abundance and service.

For most people, life is a fairly scary place ridden with fear, and we work to control and take charge of life so that tomorrow will be okay. Making sure that we save, invest, work hard, struggle, get up everyday and do something we would rather not do. We are afraid to do what we really want to do because we need to pay our bills and be able to retire…. It's a sad reality.

When we run our lives from a place of fear and lack we shrivel up, we block the flow of Grace, we remain small. Our work is to change this false notion of ourselves and to have a direct experience of the life force that sustains the Universes. The catch 22 is that this state is best accessed in the peacefulness of "being".

Instead of leading our lives trying to control the outer world, our energies are better served by getting to know, and then managing our inner world. We must first detoxify our bodies and minds to create inner healing and a clear awareness of ourselves. Not too dissimilar to a junkie going through withdrawal. Once we "get clean," everything changes and we can have a healthy, life affirming relationship with our ourselves and everyone and everything around us.

Through our practices we transmute fear into love, lack into abundance, loneliness into aloneness, surviving to thriving, sadness and depression into joy.

When we are complete unto ourselves, there is abundance in all aspects of our lives. Every relationship comes from a place of generosity and giving, as we feel no lack within ourselves. We become

Masters of our world.

Our practices allow us to tap into the Universal light force. Instead of running with a weak battery as a separated entity, we learn to plug into the Divine power grid. As this energy moves through us, it brings light into our dark places and creates deep transformations within us.

If we make the commitment and follow through, with dedication and practice, we can truly go from caterpillar to butterfly.

6

Feel your breath, listen to your heartbeat, hear your own inner music, connect to your center, and experience life from this state of being.

Cultivating Presence

Being present in every moment is one of the highest qualities you can cultivate in yourself. It is the culmination of many practices and it holds within itself knowledge, truth and the pure essence of love.

To be present is to be fully embodied in a moment of time. Your awareness is immersed in what is occurring now. Your mind is not traveling away from this moment and all of your senses are open to understanding what is actually taking place. Your mind is sitting in the unknown, experiencing the moment as it truly is.

When you are present, it is like a stilled lake, taking in and reflecting back, without distorting the beauty of each moment. Your mind is not creating ripples in the water, it is not moving ahead with projections. It is just taking it all in, deepening its perception and looking into the essence that sustains the moment.

In the stillness, you can see reality naked, unveiled, exposing your inner-connectedness and the sustaining energy of love. You can see little kids fully playing in this energy field, just for the fun of it. You can see adults lost in their own thought patterns, pulled away, separated from the pure, beautiful energy of the moment.

Life is actually happening in the present moment. When you cultivate presence, you are cultivating living. You are opening to the beauty of life, as it is.

You can spend your whole life wishing for things to be different; for someone or something to change, so that everything will be "perfect". That day will never come. Yet this day, this moment, has its own perfection which you can enjoy, if you fully embrace it and explore it.

Your mind has a tendency to reject reality for its own created fan tasy, to drift away from where it does not want to engage to its inner distorted world. By training yourself to fully engage here, you actually become empowered to engage and transform the moment. You deal with what is in front of you and by fully engaging, you begin to co-create the reality you want to experience.

Cultivating presence truly empowers you to be a co-creator of your life. By embracing and exploring every moment, you see more potential, more options allowing you to make the highest, best choices that will then manifest in the next moment of your life.

Many spiritual seekers are searching for the peak states of bliss, yet this is a very narrow range of experience. Presence of being is fully experiencing all that life has to offer with fullness and openness. Embracing sadness, sorrow, pain, as well as joy and happiness, you learn to see the love and beauty that sustains all experiences.

Presence comes from silence, from stillness, from mental focus.
It is cultivated by becoming intimate with yourself first. By developing your witness consciousness, you are able to detach enough to be able to have an experience without an automatic reaction. You are able to see and feel your inner dialogue without interfering with the moment, probing into deeper understanding, accepting the perfection of the it and choosing the best way to navigate its currents. We must take time to cultivate this state.

Our society encourages us to be "productive", to multi-task, to tackle our endless to-do-lists, to do more. It's all about quantity and not about quality.

Feel your breath, listen to your heartbeat, hear your own inner music, connect to your center, and experience life from this state of being.

7

Silence is the language of God.

MOVING TOWARDS SILENCE

Silence is achieved once we align and eliminate friction in all aspects of ourselves. So we move toward levels of silence, levels of stillness, levels of awareness.

Silence is always present underneath the noise. As we lower the quantity and volume of our distractions, we begin to enter the deeper levels of being within the silence of the present moment.

Our bodies are constantly communicating with their aches and pains when things are not in perfect alignment and optimum health. It is the movement away from the ideal that creates the noise.

Our worries, desires and fears all create a separation from being fully engaged in the present moment. This separation is the noise that distorts the stillness and beauty inherent in each moment.

In our physical yoga practice we are always moving towards creating more freedom, stability and balance. With time, our postures develop a lightness and a beauty that transports us into a whole new reality. This lack of friction, as everything comes into perfect alignment, allows our life force to move with strength, clarity, and precision creating this "lifting" feeling within ourselves. There is a tangible stillness within the movement, a silence from within that brings out an expansive expression of ourselves.

In our meditation practice we slowly move towards being more present with what is occurring within ourselves. We blend with the ebb and flow of each breath, we become observers of the workings of the mind, our focus deepens within, and we begin to experience the sounds behind the sounds, to see beyond our eyes, to know beyond our intellect. The distractions of life stay on the surface as we dive into the stillness deep within ourselves.

Rumi states that "silence is the language of God" . As we quiet the distractions of our mind/body, we enter the stillness that allows us to know our deeper spirit self. Our true nature can never leave us. However, we can bury it with all the outer noise.

Through the process of becoming more present and intimate with ourselves, through silence and contemplation, we can become aware of all the stories, distractions and misalignments that interfere with the peace and joy inherent within us. As we dive below the storms on the surface of the ocean, we can immerse ourselves in the vastness of our inner being.

We do have the ability to take the reins that control our minds. We can exercise power over our thoughts and we can align our actions to be in harmony with the life we are living. The better we know ourselves, the more influence we can have over our thoughts and actions. More control leads to more harmony, which leads to more silence which allows for more self awareness. It is a cycle that supports our spiritual evolvement.

It takes dedicated and focused effort to align and integrate in such a way that we can feel safe and secure in our lives, that we can truly know and trust that we are Divinely guided and therefore we don't need to "control" our future. We just need to be fully present to navigate, live and experience the life we are living.

8

*In skilled hands our words can be magical,
uplifting and supporting of those around us.
Co-creating an environment of respect and mutual
support, kind, loving words nourish the soul and bring
out the best in all of us.*

The Power of Our Words

There are few things more powerful than the words we use. How we express ourselves will have a great impact on others as well as on ourselves. Our words bring to life our feelings and our relationship to any given situation.

At a very simple level words are a mirror into our inner world. Words can be angry, happy, kind, thoughtful, hurtful. We can hear empathy or judgment, support or condemnation.

Words are part of our creative energy and belong to the 5th chakra, the blue throat of Shiva. Words are a physical, vibrational representation of thoughts and feelings. They are a bridge from our inner world to the outer world and are a major component of the creation process. With every statement we make, we are affirming a belief, we are making a stand, we are telling the Universe what our truths are.

We all have negative thoughts. We can be unsure of things. We have many opposing dialogues within ourselves as we process any situation but when we speak, we are affirming to the world a belief of how things are and that is what the world will create for us to experience.

Our spiritual practices support our efforts to create a more loving and peaceful world. Through mindfulness we become more aware of our thoughts and of our words. We have an opportunity to bring a more positive outlook into whatever experience we are living. By looking for the good and expressing that goodness in our words, we will create a better world for ourselves and those around us.

There are many things in our lives that are out of our control, but we do have total control of every word that comes out of our mouths. And if we can't find positive words for a given situation, we always have the ability to say nothing, to not affirm a negative.

In unskilled hands our words can do tremendous damage. They can become the negative inner dialogue of a child; not being good enough, not being worthy. A loved one, in their ignorance, can destroy our self-worth, our self-esteem. Those words, placed inside our minds, we will repeat about ourselves, deepening that "false-truth" to both ourselves and the Universe.

In skilled hands our words can be magical, uplifting and supporting of those around us. Co-creating an environment of respect and mutual support, kind, loving words nourish the soul and bring out the best in all of us.

Being observant about what we say about ourselves allows us to create the best and highest version of our lives. If we beat ourselves up with our words, life will beat us up. If we affirm the positive in ourselves, that will blossom in our lives.

Words are extremely powerful and they can be used equally for good or for bad. They can damage or they can heal, and we have total control of every single word that comes out of our mouths. Be mindful, become skillful of this amazing force within and make the highest choice always!

9

By refining our own being, we are in an empowered position from which to engage with life.

THE COLORS WE CARRY

We tend to be worried about all the things we cannot control. Therefore, we don't need to worry or control these things. We also tend to pay very little attention to the things we actually can and should control, mainly, the colors, the vibration we carry.

We are entities fundamentally composed of molecules moving in wavelike form in space and time. We have physical, mental, emotional and energetic bodies creating a certain vibration, which is the primary way in which we interact and communicate with the world. The words we say are only about 15% of how we communicate. We really speak with a vibrational voice.

Just like we have one of a kind fingerprints, we are also completely unique in the vibration we carry. There is no one else in the Universe just like you!

If we have our thoughts, feelings and actions all in agreement, there is integrity, which leads to clarity and purpose in our being. We clearly express what we desire and very directly move to manifest it. If we have competing messages between these different parts of our being, there is no clarity nor force with which to manifest into reality.

By creating greater integration, harmony, and alignment of our bodies, we can refine our vibration and create a higher state of wellbeing for ourselves and those around us. We can choose the "feeling state" we would like to be in, and we can choose to hold the feeling state on all our different bodies, (emotional, mental, physical). Both of these actions are what we can truly actively control.

Therefore our primary focus is to be placed on our "being" state. Instead of looking to control the outer world, we can work on controlling the quality of our breath, our thoughts, our actions and our emotions. By refining our own being, we are in an empowered position from which to engage with life. We create a place of clarity, integrity and precision which easily blends with the reality of the present moment. As we and the outer world come into alignment, friction and conflict are eliminated from our lives. A state of inner peace and harmony is created.

If we set time aside each day to tend to our own wellbeing, we will be creating a profound change not only in ourselves, but it will also ripple out to the whole world. All change starts from within and the practices are fairly simple. It takes desire, time, and effort to develop the mental focus, the inner-knowing, awareness and mindfulness to become fully empowered, to feel the quality of our vibration, and to reflect the colors we are carrying.

Our outer world is only a reflection of our inner world. Peace, health, love, happiness, joy, abundance, etc. are all created from within. Spending our days in fear and anxiety over our uncertain future is a futile path.

As we develop this inner strength and grounding, life becomes this beautiful adventure to explore and experience. We welcome every day with the enthusiasm and delight of a child ready to explore the gifts inherent in each moment. The outer landscape changes but our inner being remains constant and vibrant.

10

*Start your day with gratitude and be inquisitive of
what gifts are waiting to be unwrapped
by fully engaging in each moment, as it is.*

Every Day Starts as a Blank Slate

I have the "habit" of staying in bed every morning for just a few extra minutes to be thankful for the many small and large blessings that are in my life. I allow myself to experience a positive connection with the life I am living, which sets the tone for my day.

Each sunrise gives a blank slate in which to engage with the world around us. Life is just happening, dogs bark, birds fly, people are moving around doing their thing. We are both witnesses and participants in the activities of our days. We have the power and responsibility to make conscious choices of how we will engage with the day and those around us.

If we focus on the things we feel we are lacking, we will create a 'not good enough' mindset and our day, our life, will simply not be fun. Our life will have the feeling that something is lacking, while in reality every moment is perfectly complete. Just because there are things in our day that we would not place there and other things that we want are missing, does not make the day any less perfect. Our skill lies in navigating the day that has been given to us. Accepting its inherent perfection and fully engaging with it to receive all the gifts and teachings that it has to offer.

Only by fully accepting and engaging with the "light and shadow" sides of our experience, are we in a position to co-create a different reality for the future. The actions of today will set the path for what we will experience tomorrow. Hoping or wishing for a things to be different is not enough. We make decisions and take action in the present moment that will bear fruit at the appropriate time. The first change must come from within ourselves.

I love the complexity of our being. We can focus on the little things, the big picture or somewhere in between. Having a big picture frame that reminds us that there is a harmony and perfection in the grand scheme of things. The sun rises in the East and sets in the West every single day. Birds migrate within the harmony of the seasons. There is this intelligence, a life source that is, and sustains the whole Universe. Being aware that we are intricately connected in this fabric of consciousness expressing itself, allows us to embrace the day as it comes. We can look for the beauty, the teachings, and the blessings in every moment.

Start your day with gratitude and be inquisitive of what gifts are waiting to be unwrapped by fully engaging in each moment, as it is.

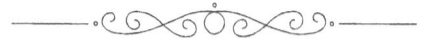

11

Birds of the same feather fly together

THE IMPORTANCE OF RIGHT COMPANY

All wisdom traditions and religions emphasize community in some way. The Catholic Parish, Yoga Kula, and Buddhist Shanga are all meant to cultivate a sense of unity, shared values, and a way of being in the world.

Our cultural sayings also point to a similar truth; "birds of the same feather fly together" and "tell me who your friends are and I'll tell you who you are".

I like to think of this from the perspective of energy and resonance which is the way in which the Universe organizes things. We have attraction, repulsion, and neutrality to people, situations and things. Someone we don't know may enter a crowded room and we will feel a connection without knowing why. It might be an attraction or a repulsion, strong or weak, but there is something in them that we intuitively feel in ourselves, and then we use our minds to analyze and interpret what that is.

As we start spiritual practices we begin to change our energy, our vibration, our resonance. We practice to connect with deeper levels of our own being. These levels offer us a sense of peace and well-being, a harmony and integrity within ourselves, and they slowly polish and change us.

Many times our eating habits will change. We begin to find new activities that we now prefer and new people whose company we enjoy. These changes, many times, can cause discomfort with our partners and our old friends. We are changing and they are used to the old us. Subconsciously and energetically a new relationship has to be created that takes into account who we are becoming. During these transition periods, there may be friction with old friends and a sense that they are attempting to prevent this transformation.

It is really helpful to receive the support of spending time and being with people who are also on the path. They are doing the work to shift and refine their own being and are vibrating at the higher vibration that you are also working to acquire and maintain. They will understand your challenges, support your efforts, applaud your changes.

(Over these many years at the Yoga Center we have created a very peaceful, respectful, and supportive community of practitioners. There is grounded spiritual energy cultivated through years of dedicated practice, which can be easily felt upon entering. It is a sanctuary holding an energy that will support your inner growth. Come and see how your being feels within our walls).

12

*Just like the Sun,
we can fully share our light with others knowing that
the source of our light comes from within.*

LIFE IS AN INSIDE JOB

The things that matter the most in our lives are only attainable by the qualities we bring to each situation. It is by the way we perceive life that we can truly partake and enjoy the full rainbow of gifts that it offers.

Most of us spend our time looking at the outer landscape of our lives; what we have externally acquired and what is left to conquer; how successful we have become based on society's definition of success. When we value and compare ourselves through the lens of the outer world there can be a feeling of lack and a never ending hunger for more.

The actual feelings of love, joy, abundance, safety, contentment, peace, freedom, etc., have very little to do with the actual circumstances of our lives and all to do with how we have cultivated those qualities within ourselves.

We can be alone and not feel lonely, we can have a substantial trust fund and be fearful of our security. The outer circumstances have very little to do with how we actually feel about any given situation.

This cultivation of true well being is the key to our personal and societal health and balance. When we look outside ourselves to satisfy our feelings and emotions we are heading in the wrong direction. By exploring our feelings in deep meditation and contemplation, we can see how they are manufactured by our unconscious beliefs. Only by looking deeply and soberly into our fears and challenges can we fully embrace them, and therefore be in a position to transmute them into a positive force in our lives.

Our fears and challenges are nothing but paper tigers in our minds projected into our uncertain future. Left unchecked they will distort our very existence and steal the beauty that is present in every moment.

I am not saying that there are no real fears or dangers, for we can certainly find ourselves in perilous circumstances. In these situations we need to take clear and precise actions to protect ourselves and those around us. But even in these more extreme circumstances the available options we will perceive, will be determined by the state of our minds. Fear and anxiety will tremendously diminish our ability to perceive what is actually occurring and the potential options for moving forward.

By taking time everyday to become more connected and intimate with ourselves is how we cultivate our inner landscape. The only person that will be with you from birth to death is yourself. Explore and discover all the layers of your own being and find the bounty that lives within. Everything we really need and can truly satisfy us lies within.

There is an inner universe to be explored and a place within ourselves that contains all those precious qualities we want to own and express in our lives. All of existence lives within us.

Living life from this inner place of true abundance is how we can become a light in this world. Imagine not "needing" anything. Instead we will be in a position to give freely, love without attachment, enjoy each moment with what it truly offers.

Just like the Sun, we can fully share our light with others knowing that the source of our light comes from within.

13

Holding steady in your desires and consistent in your actions, you can co-create your hearts' longings.

CO-CREATE YOUR LIFE

Take charge of your life and make your dreams come true. Don't fall into the victim trap feeling that you are small and powerless.

Every single day you can make small decisions that start to move you in the direction that you would like to go. Each step in the right direction begins to draw forth the support of the Universe. If something is of interest begin to explore it. If something does not feel right, starve it by withdrawing your attention.

You are the master of your world, and by giving or withdrawing your energy/attention, you navigate the direction of your life. Don't live unconscious of your power because you are always co-creating your reality either by default or by intent.

Every journey begins with an intent and then a small amount of action. Holding steady in your desires and consistent in your actions, you can co-create your hearts longings.

No one, nor any situation has the power to stop you. Only your limiting thoughts and beliefs keep you small and stuck. Don't look outside of yourself for answers.

Listen for your heart's desires and take small steps toward bringing that feeling, that experience, you wish to have. Your heart is magical and like a compass it points to your true north. Your mind is logical and contains knowledge. Follow the wisdom of the heart and use your mind to create a path toward your destiny.

Hold steady to your vision, invite grace to pave the way, and enjoy the magical journey as it unfolds before you!

14

*Love begins
with the direct experience of loving ourselves,
accepting all aspects of our complicated being
and knowing we are an expression of Divine light.*

Experiencing Love

So much has been written on love with so many potential facets of expression. From the passion of lovers, to a mother's protection of her child, to a martyr's love for a cause that places his life below that glorified cause.

All of these are expressions of the energy of love through the distortions of "maya", the illusion of life. These are expressions of love wrapped up in need, lack, fear, attachments, and ignorance.

Love must be experienced from our own connection to our Divine self. Love is a state of being beyond the cravings of the mind. Only out of the fullness and completeness of our own being can we truly be in a state of love.

When there are no needs, we can give freely, just for the joy that it will create in others. No recognition required, no strings attached. A gift is just a gift. It can not be a binding contract between the giver and the receiver.

Love begins with the direct experience of loving ourselves, accepting all aspects of our complicated being and knowing we are an expression of Divine light. Once we know that in ourselves, we are then able to see it in others. Acceptance and compassion for our fellow man is just a natural extension of this awareness.

Through our spiritual practices, we are able to clear out the distortions in our perception of needs and separation and come to a place of becoming our own best friend; to know that we are whole and complete in our own being; that each moment contains within itself all we actually need, and that our wants are simply a non-acceptance of the perfection of each moment.

We have the pattern of remaining with the thoughts of our minds instead of exploring the fullness of the present moment. Once we train ourselves to make that shift we connect to the source that sustains the Universe and a profound level of peace, stillness and love emerges. From this place we are able to know love, to share fully, to be open completely to life.

We are surrounded by love, yet we don't tend to take the time to perceive it. Every breath, every flower, every tree, every raindrop, and every ray of sunlight is an act of love. Fully engaging in what is happening in each moment is the gateway to a state of being connected to Divine reality, being in love.

Until we have experienced contentment with our own being, all of our relationships will be conditional in nature. If we look for someone to complete us we are entering a co-dependent, need based arrangement.

Once we are contented from within, we are in a place to fully share, fully give, and fully engage just for the joy of it. We are able to love someone as they are, with their perfect imperfections. We give our partners the freedom to be themselves. We give ourselves the freedom to engage in ways that are life affirming and to walk away without judgments from situations that don't feel right for us. No one has to be right or wrong, it is just a matter of wether we would like to have that experience or not.

Inherent in love is a respect for the uniqueness in all of us; an ability to listen for the sake of understanding a different perspective than ours. A taking of responsibility for our own well-being. An understanding and respect for the choices others are making.

Love is the opposite of fear. Once we are contented, non-fearful, non-needy, we can truly be in the energy of pure Love.

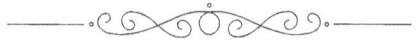

15

Slowing down enough to learn to appreciate the beauty and quality of all that surrounds us, is critical for a happy and fulfilled life.

Quality vs Quantity

In our consumer driven society we have been programmed into believing that more is always better. If something is good then having more of it would be great. We super size our meals, have multiple homes, multiple cars, even multiple lovers. We need to have the next big job, the next big exotic vacation. Always looking for the next "high" experience. Hikers start counting how many peaks they have climbed. Even spiritual seekers get caught up looking for the next "peak" experience.

All of this quantity is our way of looking to feel good, to feel satisfied, and contented. Somehow we think this makes us "good enough". This is like the hamster in its cage going around in circles and never going anywhere.

In reality, the more things that we own, the heavier our lives becomes because we are now responsible for them. They actually own us!

Slowing down enough to learn to appreciate the beauty and quality of all that surrounds us, is critical for a happy and fulfilled life. We all need our basic needs meet; food, shelter, clothing, connection to others, a place to belong in society. Beyond the basics it becomes a matter of choice and we need to see what is driving those choices.

For example, our bodies need a certain amount and quality of food.

If we over feed our bodies we end up with a lot of health issues. Finding moderation is the key to life. Unblocking mental and emotional distortions that lead to over consumption, is something we all need to explore.

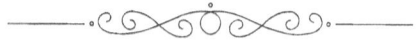

16

*As we find our inner compass
and loosen the outer limitations,
we become direct expressions of our soul's light.*

15

Slowing down enough to learn to appreciate the beauty and quality of all that surrounds us, is critical for a happy and fulfilled life.

QUALITY VS QUANTITY

In our consumer driven society we have been programmed into believing that more is always better. If something is good then having more of it would be great. We super size our meals, have multiple homes, multiple cars, even multiple lovers. We need to have the next big job, the next big exotic vacation. Always looking for the next "high" experience. Hikers start counting how many peaks they have climbed. Even spiritual seekers get caught up looking for the next "peak" experience.

All of this quantity is our way of looking to feel good, to feel satisfied, and contented. Somehow we think this makes us "good enough". This is like the hamster in its cage going around in circles and never going anywhere.

In reality, the more things that we own, the heavier our lives becomes because we are now responsible for them. They actually own us!

Slowing down enough to learn to appreciate the beauty and quality of all that surrounds us, is critical for a happy and fulfilled life. We all need our basic needs meet; food, shelter, clothing, connection to others, a place to belong in society. Beyond the basics it becomes a matter of choice and we need to see what is driving those choices.

For example, our bodies need a certain amount and quality of food.

If we over feed our bodies we end up with a lot of health issues. Finding moderation is the key to life. Unblocking mental and emotional distortions that lead to over consumption, is something we all need to explore.

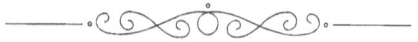

16

*As we find our inner compass
and loosen the outer limitations,
we become direct expressions of our soul's light.*

Creative Expression

The highest expression of ourselves is achieved by allowing our creative energy to flow unimpeded.

We are unique expressions of the Divine. Not only are our fingerprints unique, but really every aspect of our being is an original expression. We carry a frequency, a vibration that gives us a unique relationship with life. We see, feel, understand, and express as only we can.

We all have the same body parts and yet we all move, eat, walk, in unique ways; we live within our bodies with a very personal expression.

Its interesting that there is an outer pressure to conform to a way of being, that really does not fully fit anyone. This "one size fits all" world is a crazy idea. Creative expression comes when we begin to create a life that is custom made, tailor fitted, to support our own unique highest expression.

Our job is not to align to the currents of the outer world, but to delve into the layers of our inner world, to discover and honor our inner rhythm and knowing. The rules of the outer world are set to benefit the power structure, to keep us like sheep, being herded in the way that benefits the power elite.

This set-up keeps us small and restricted. Some folks, literally lose their souls to succeed within these outer driven parameters, and others feel like failures because this way of being does not work for them. If we compare and judge ourselves to the successes and abilities of others, this again creates another fundamental misalignment of our energies.

Life is not a competition. We all start and end in the same place, and yet we all have a one of a kind journey to experience in between those two set points. It is our birthright and responsibility to break out of the societal confines and to live an authentic life, embracing all our gifts and challenges to have the most amazing life experience.

Our creative expressions come from cultivating a sense of confidence in ourselves. That sense of confidence can be enhanced by deepening our embodiment, by connecting to our gentle inner voice, by connecting to our own inner rhythm. We move from having an external point of reference to an internal sense of being.

As we find our inner compass and loosen the outer limitations we become direct expressions of our soul's light. We align to our life's journey and move with the force of inner passion and Divine expression.

To be creative, by definition, means doing something new, original. It means going beyond common knowledge and bringing forth an original expression. It means bringing forth that uniqueness that lives within us, as our self.

The more authentic we can be, the more creative our lives will become. To be authentic, we must embody a certain level of safety and self acceptance, which will give us the freedom to be ourselves.

17

Every challenge that comes our way brings with it an opportunity for growth, just as every gift that comes to us brings with it challenge and responsibility.

Following Grace

What would happen if instead of trying to change the situation we are in, we actually let it change us? Can we embrace each moment in awe of its perfection and look to see what it is offering to teach us? Can we feel our fear, our loneliness, our unfulfilled desires, and pierce through them by going fearlessly into our experience?

We live in a culture that thinks that if we are not happy, something is wrong…. Feeling sad, maybe we should take a pill to avoid the unpleasant feelings we are having? Our culture chooses to place a band aid on anything that feels uncomfortable. It wants to hide what we are here to experience in order to grow and transform into who we are to become.

Literally, mind-blowing transformation comes as we navigate through the dark nights of the soul. Having to question our beliefs, letting go of our attachments, and moving into our fears, is how the fire of transformation works. Life is not for the faint of heart! Our virtues are cultivated by our experiences. Most of our "heroes" had very difficult life experiences which helped them become the people we now admire.

If we understand, if we know, that every experience is here in support of our growth, we can fully embrace each moment. Troubles arrive when we choose to push away, not accept, and argue with what has been given to us. Grace will support us as we face every challenge with humility and openness. She will work her magic of inner-transformation that will be reflected in both inner and outer changes that are truly magical.

In no way am I saying that we should stay stuck in a bad situation and take it as our destiny. I am saying that every situation brings with it a lesson to be explored, and when we master the lesson, we will be released from that situation. Denial or avoidance of our experience simply delays our growth and keeps us small.

Every challenge that comes our way brings with it an opportunity for growth, just as every gift that comes to us brings with it challenge and responsibility. By its very nature, the manifested world is dense, has restrictions, gives us a sense of separation, and is full of physical, mental, and emotional challenges. By embracing its nature and knowing that we are here to grow from these experiences, we can learn to surf through this terrain. We can align ourselves with Grace and embrace all that comes our way.

Through the process of accepting, developing an understanding, and working through the solutions of our challenges, we transform knowledge into wisdom and we become masters of our lives.

18

Aligning, trusting, actively surrendering, and flowing with this life force is how we become our greatest expression of Divine light.

THE LIGHT WITHIN

There is an intelligence, a creative and expressive force, working through all of existence. It is what organizes energy and molecules into existence, what guides a seed into becoming a tree. Nothing moves, nothing exists, without this life force containing it.

This same light lives within us and expresses itself through us. It flows through the openings that we allow it to have based on our beliefs. We filter how much light moves through us by our limiting thoughts. The light that lives within us will support us in any way we allow it to flow through us. It is called Free Will.

Any time we say "I am…" we are guiding how this infinite light will come to expression in and around us. The conscious and unconscious thoughts and beliefs are guiding all that we will become, all that we will experience.

This light, in its pure form, is love, felt as joy, experienced as abundance and contentment. This light has no opposite, no polarity from which to judge. It just flows through our whole universe expressing itself as all that there is.

Our job is to allow as much of that light to flow through us in its purest form. Through our spiritual practices, we are able to have a more direct experience of that force, allowing it to become more "real" in our belief system. We can allow that light to express itself through us more fully by consciously aligning ourselves with it.

Fear, judgement, separation, control, all limit our potential. Aligning, trusting, actively surrendering, and flowing with this life force is how we become our greatest expression of Divine light.

Our small ego-selves are what restricts the flow... Invite them to experience the energy that created it and sustains it. Look within to the source that birthed us and continue to evolve and express it into our full potential.

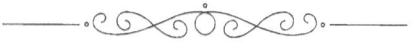

19

The change we want begins within ourselves, managing our thoughts, emotions and actions to create inner peace and stillness.

A Reflecting Pond

There is a direct connection within our state of mind and the circumstances of our outer world. They are reflections of each other. More precisely, what we experience externally is a direct reflection of our thoughts and feelings.

When we are conflicted inside with what is occurring in our outer world there is tension with reality, a non- acceptance, judgment, and separation with what is. It is a state of ignorance (not understanding) and separation from the Divine flow.

Our words and our actions show that internal state of our being. When we "hate" something, when we are "hurt" by someone, when we feel we need to "fight" for things to occur, those are all signals of us feeling separate from the Divine flow.

When the mind is at peace we have a more detached perspective with the outer world. We are able to have compassion for others, have a broader perspective on any given situation. We are not "needy" of things to be a certain way. Feeling safe, there is very little need to control.

The change we want begins within ourselves, managing our thoughts, emotions and actions to create inner peace and stillness. With internal and external harmony, our energy is freed-up and can be used to inspire and support others. We can fertilize the world with love, compassion and understanding.

We can become that beautiful, still pond reflecting the good and harmonious nature that surrounds us. To embody, peace, love and harmony is our highest calling.

20

Our practices make a profound change in our physical, mental, and emotional bodies.

Practice Leads to Transformation

Our yoga and meditation practices are designed to create lasting and profound changes in us from the inside out. They slowly change how we relate with our own being and with the outer world.

I was talking to a student that has had a consistent practice for about six months, and she was joking with me about how she could no longer deal with her rambunctious neighbor…they used to be good friends, but she was having a hard time putting up with her bad habits and could no longer just let them slide.

I had a good idea where this was coming from, so I asked, "Are there other things you can no longer put up with, other changes you've begun to make?" Her eyes lit up! Yes, and she started listing one after another the unhealthy things she had changed because she no longer wanted them for herself. These were not conscious, precipitated choices. They came from a lack of tolerance to things and people that were of a lower vibration.

The more peace and harmony we cultivate within ourselves, the greater the contrast and the more uncomfortable it is to be with people and situations that are not holding this integrity, similar to taking a quiet walk on a country road and all of a sudden someone comes by blasting their music. They are welcome to listen to whatever they like… just don't make me listen to it!

Our practices make a profound change in our physical, mental, and emotional bodies. They bring a sense of embodiment, inner peace, contentment, and well-being. We become more intimate with who we really are and what brings us peace and joy. This changes us!

Once we embody the practice, there is very little desire or tolerance for drama, unhealthy foods or drinks, or disharmony of any kind.

21

True freedom comes from liberating our mind by training it to be stilled and silent.

Moment, to Moment, to Moment

Have you noticed how difficult it is to keep our minds from drifting in all sorts of directions? In the practice of meditation, it is described as trying to herd cats, or puppy mind.

Many of us live with untrained minds that are just running wild without any control. Our minds are so wild that many folks don't even know they are wild! There is no understanding of the root of their emotions, or the total lack of harmony living within themselves.

Most of us have obsessions, addictions to our work, kids, drugs, sex, exercise… to almost anything that our mind highlights to pull us from the present moment. Always interpreting things, taking us to past experiences, or into the unforeseeable future. Restlessly disturbing the peace inherent in this moment. These patterns are so strong that many folks have a very difficult time simply being quiet and still.

Just like any addiction, we need to break away from it! We replace these energy draining, unhealthy habits by working out our mental muscles to cultivate presence in the present moment. We can create mental pathways that gently begin to take us back, moment by moment, into what is truly occurring.

We are not our thoughts. We have a mind, but we are not the thoughts that the mind creates. These thoughts are the interpretations and imaginations of our minds, based on past experiences being projected into the future. They keep us trapped, prejudging and highjacking every experience.

True freedom comes from liberating our mind by training it to be stilled and silent.

Beyond the noise of the mind is the peace and stillness of awareness.

22

*Our state of inner harmony,
becomes a guiding force in the choices we make.*

INNER HARMONY

Take time every single day to arrive at a place of inner harmony, even if it is for just a minute.

There are always things that we can be doing, that we can worry about, that we can try to control, and plenty of things to obsess about. This is what we do almost every moment of our lives in some sort of way. It is our habitual pattern.

It takes commitment and practice to bring ourselves on a consistent basis, to a place of stillness and inner harmony. That is why spiritual practices are called "practice." We need to repeat them in a consistent way in order to receive their benefits.

There are many timeless techniques to bring us into the experience of the present moment; To yoke, bind, connect in a moment of time, our mind, body and spirit. This connection creates integrity and wholeness in us. It changes our normal state of feeling separated, with all of its negative side effects.

With time and practice we get used to anchoring the experience of each moment by being aware of our own breath. By minimizing outer stimuli we can sense our own inner rhythm. Once we are accustomed to our state of inner harmony, there will be little tolerance for people or situations that disturb us and it becomes a guiding force in the choices we make…. Each choice affirming a life that is in harmony and integrity.

23

*Fall in love with the light
that lives through you, as you.*

Self-Love / Self-Acceptance

Spiritual practice is meant to bring us into greater intimacy and relationship with ourselves. Instead of moving away from our own being, with self-judgments, we must embrace our uniqueness and appreciate the gifts that it offers to us and the world.

Our patterns, habits of maintaining an outer reference point and perspective, makes us quite judgmental. We are truly looking in the wrong place for all that we are searching for. It is just fundamentally backwards!

Practicing awareness and exploration of our bodies, our thoughts, our emotions, our breath, leads us to a better understanding of our own uniqueness…There has never been, nor will there ever be, another human being just like you. To compare and compete with one another is such a crazy ego concept. We are here to shine our own individual light, and in doing so, we help each other move towards our highest expression of our true nature.

Understand yourself, explore how your body moves, and with practice, bring elegance and poise into your physical being. Understand how your mind works, know the personality you have created, and refine your ego so that it can support the work you came here to do… the work of the soul.

The more masterful you become of your own being, the greater the expression of your Divine light that will shine forth. If you truly know yourself, you will undoubtably feel acceptance and love for the perfectly imperfect being that you are.

Develop your potential with tender love. Our treasure lies within. Become your confidante, your best friend. Fall in love with the light that lives through you, as you.

24

True happiness comes from your ability to be "authentically you".

Fundamentals

As humans we have this amazing ability to complicate things. It's like we look to fill in empty space with lots of noise and clutter, so much so, that we lose track of the simplicity that life actually is.

When we are born, we are basically given a body from which to experience life, and a mind from which to create and discern the life that is occurring around us. Our soul comes with a life purpose to fulfill and explore. At the most basic level, we are only responsible for feeding and sheltering the body so that it continues to function. Yet, at that same basic level, we also have an innate desire to express our creative energy, and to be in relationship with life and others, to belong.

In our outward-focused world we forget how simple our needs really are and we think that to be fulfilled we must acquire many items, fill our brains with earthly facts, and create a "societally defined successful persona" to become worthy.

We tend to associate happiness with physical possessions and status, and yet, true happiness comes from our ability to be "authentically you". To express our own unique light and creativity is living our dharma, being fully aligned with our life purpose and journey.

In Yoga, life is described as a "mirage, an illusion," where we chase shadows outside of ourselves. Always searching and never arriving, we are caught up in all the glitter and emptiness of the outer search.

How many homes do you need to shelter your body? How much clothing do you need to stay warm and dry? How much outer success do you need to feel worthy? Use your energy to express your deepest desires, to follow your dreams, to live your dharma. De-stress your life by lightening your load and acquire the most precious of all commodities…TIME.

We are traveling through time. Keep things simple and light, enjoy the ebb and flow of the journey, and allow life to unfold on its own Divine Timing. Our greatest responsibility is to remain true to ourselves and to live our highest version.

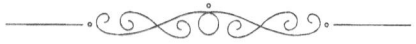

25

Notice the drama in which some people choose to engage with life and know that there is an opposite place that you can inhabit that is quiet, peaceful, harmonious and genuine.

Beyond Emotions

We spend most of our lives with a gentle, or not so gentle impulse that we must do something. That there is something pending that we must take care of or the whole world will come crashing down! There are currents of feelings, some conscious and others unconscious, that tell us that things are not right just the way they are, and that we must do something about it.

With our spiritual practices we can move beyond these subtle emotions and enter a world of real stillness and contentment. We can quiet that inner voice that has fear and judgement and move to a place of contemplation and acceptance.

There is an empty place within us, a void, that holds pure presence. A place that holds no drama, nor attachments. It simply enjoys the moment as it is. Not too dissimilar to a tree which is fully alive and ever present. Never reacting, but always responding to the ebb and flow of the seasons and the path of the sun.

The yogis call all our emotions, attachments, fears and drama, "Maya", described as the illusions of life. It is the distortions our minds place over what is actually occurring in the present moment. Life is just happening. How we feel about what is occurring is our own personal distortion. This noisy and distorted interpretation is what creates all of our challenges and brings stress into our lives.

Notice how family, friends and co-workers live in their version of reality. Notice the drama in which some people choose to engage with life and know that there is an opposite place that you can inhabit that is quiet, peaceful, harmonious and genuine. All that is required is your intent and dedication to cultivate this within yourself. The tools are many, the path is well lit, and there is nothing external that you need to purchase or acquire. It is your choice to make.

26

Every situation comes with opportunities for growth and transformation.

Free Will: The Human Experience

The human species has a very special characteristic that allows us to be co-creators of our own lives. Simply put, we have the option to align to a highest good or not. As the world is happening around us, we get to decide how to relate to it. This decision is both conscious and unconscious, as it it driven by our perceptions and beliefs.

If you look at other life on the planet, it is mostly guided by instincts and a natural alignment to the energy and seasons of Mother Earth. We can choose to be stupid, to go against nature, to create havoc, to let fear and discontentment run our lives, or we can choose to align to the natural intelligence that holds harmony in the whole universe. The choice is quite simple.

We are kings & queens of our own lives. We have the power to create any reality we wish to experience. What we make important, what we give our attention to, will manifest. Our worries and fears will come to life, as well as our love and our joy. Our work is to cultivate the qualities we want to experience inside ourselves so that they can manifest in our outer world.

Yoga states that we have personal freedom to bind and unbind ourselves from anyone or anything as we move through life. That quality is Svatantrya, the weaving and unweaving of the fabric of our lives.

Take responsibility for the state of your personal kingdom and make the choices and changes that will take you to a place of inner peace and joy. Every situation comes with opportunities for growth and transformation. You are only a victim if you choose to see yourself as one.

We are powerful beyond belief. The life you are living is of your own creation. Be wise and manifest a life worth living!

27

We hold the key to our own freedom.

The Gate Keeper

Our mind is the gate keeper between the outer reality and God's vast universe. Our ego-mind keeps us busy and engaged in the drama of life. It creates lots of noise and holds us trapped in our emotions, especially those founded in fear. It endlessly creates problems and feelings for us to solve, keeping us like a gerbil running in circles.

Having created a false sense of separation from the Divine force that sustains the Universe, we begin to function in survival mode, trying to control our outer world. The minute we identify with our ego-self, we have lost the knowledge of our True-self. We experience life as separate and lacking.

Our consciousness can sit in our ego-mind or our soul identity. It can actually easily move between both of those realities to allow us the experience of being in the world, and also the knowledge that we are much more than earthly beings.

When we sit in our ego identity we can only experience and relate to a very small range of what is in existence. We are like a radio that can only tune to one station and we are completely sure that nothing else exists because we have not experienced it.

As we cultivate our ability to witness and silence the mind, our consciousness moves away from total identification with our ego-identity and it becomes free to explore the vast inner universe that is our True-self.

Not too dissimilar to disrobing, we start looking at the stories and sense of self that we have placed on our being, and gently start taking them off. Once we shed those outer layers and are naked in our stillness and being-ness, we have direct awareness of our infinite nature. We hold the key to our own freedom.

28

The world we experience is of our own making.

It's Not What We Do,
But How We Do It That Truly Matters

We are here to develop inner qualities of our being, to refine ourselves as one would polish a stone. The more refined we become, the more beautiful the light is reflected in us, through us.

We spend too much time worrying about outer aspects of our lives. Pondering about our ideal job, the best place to live, or that perfect partner. Those things are much less important than focusing on how we are interacting in the job we have, and how we relate to the community in which we live. Look at the quality of our friendships and the gifts of our relationships.

Do we engage with our world from a place of fear, anger, control? Are we in a place of openness, love, and joy with our environment? Wherever we go, there we are. The grass is truly not greener on the other side of the fence. The world we experience is of our own making.

How we relate to the outer world is a reflection of how we relate to ourselves. If you have love, compassion, and acceptance of our own being, then we will have that for others. If we are grounded and connected to our deepest self, we will enjoy the uniqueness of others.

Take time everyday for practices that cultivate the inner peace that is the foundation for our true growth and evolution. Walking in nature, yoga, meditation, time for rest, and contemplation are necessary for our physical and psychological well-being.

Wherever we are in our lives at this moment, is the perfect place to begin an inner journey of discovery and transformation. These internal baby steps will bring the outer fruits we desire.

29

A radical revolution is waiting within you.

Yoga's Purpose & Power

The original teachings of Yoga, handed down by Saints and Masters, were for the total liberation of our ego's cycle of life, death, and reincarnation.

Over the last hundred years we have separated Yoga from its primary intention and looked at only its positive side benefits. Some do Yoga for its physical benefits, others for stress release… the typical comment is, "I like how I feel after class." This is all well and good, except that we are leaving behind 95% of its potential.

We are using Yoga to help us function slightly better in this incredibly dysfunctional world. We use it therapeutically for all that ails us. We have a very watered down use for this gift from the Sages.

Yoga is about total transformation and liberation. It is revolution that brings down the tyranny of the ego-mind and gives us direct connection to our higher soul being. It is here to break us free from our constant state of fear and separation and bring us to a state of being that is at rest in love and harmony with all there is. Don't settle for anything less!

The mystics and great teachers of all our religions speak of this state of being. The yogis created a detailed path for attaining it. The highest truth is the same. Each master describes his particular journey and experience within this enlightened state.

A radical revolution is waiting within you that will bring Heaven to Earth. The change comes from within and its calling you to come home, to move beyond the distortions of your outer desires to the stillness and deep joy that lives within you.

30

Once we move beyond this limited experience of ourselves, we can connect with the fullness of our immortal soul, the true essence of ourselves.

The Enlightened Ego

Our goal as modern day spiritual beings is to have a healthy and functional ego that is fully aware and integrated with our deeper spiritual side.

Many times, meditation is taught as going beyond the ego. There is a sense that we must eliminate our human identity to reach the higher levels of ourselves. That is not true. By incorporating the truth of who we really are into our identity, we can continue to be in this world with the harmony of true Knowledge.

The ego identity is part of our being, as is our body and mind. There is also a vast universe that dances and expresses itself through us that is us.

We tend to only see one branch of a majestic tree that holds thousands of branches. As our ego becomes aware that it is the whole tree being expressed as that branch, it can enjoy the fullness of its' true identity. In the same manner, we tend only to see this one lifetime; Once we move beyond this limited experience of ourselves, we can connect with the fullness of our immortal soul, the true essence of ourselves.

An enlightened ego rests in the knowledge that it is part of the whole universe. Pure light and love sustain its existence. It surrenders its small self to fully experience the joy and bliss of the Divine dancing within. It releases its false sense of control and rides the waves of life for the sheer pleasure of experience.

See in each moment the gift and perfection that it offers. Everyday has something special, its own unique quality. Align, enjoy, and explore all that comes your way. Let it move through you as you, staying centered and grounded in the knowledge of your True Self.

31

Tending to all the different needs of our human being is what creates the beautiful life we all wish to experience.

Tending Our Garden

In order to stay mentally, emotionally, and physically healthy, we need to take care of ourselves. Everyday, we need to tend to our needs in a mindful and knowledgeable way.

I had a backyard that I did not use with just a small amount of grass. Too small for a lawnmower and too large for a weed whacker, I began to ignore it. In no time at all, the whole backyard was a total mess. Everything overgrown…It was a disaster!

In the same way, our spiritual practices and awareness help keep us growing in a healthy way. There is no stopping growth, but it does need to be managed or we will end up with quite a mess.

Making our well-being a priority allows us to become a truly beautiful expression of the Divine. We must be fertilized, watered, pruned, and weeds must be removed or they will take over.

We are not machines to be run into the ground. We have been given a beautiful body that needs attention and care. We have a very powerful mind that interprets, and co-creates our life. We have the inner wisdom of our soul that is our responsibility to express. Tending to all the different needs of our human being is what creates the beautiful life we all wish to experience. If we neglect any part of ourselves, we will have blemishes, brown spots, and weeds in our being.

We must take time to nourish the soul. Our bodies need to be properly fed and exercised, and our minds need to rest, as well as be challenged. Learning to listen to the wisdom of the mind and body, giving it what it needs, is of the upmost importance.

Our attention can not be placed solely on the outer demands of life. Focusing on our well-being creates the foundation for an empowered, healthy, and fulfilling life.

32

*Allow love to move freely
through every cell of your being.
Feel its energy as it dances with you,
through you, as you.*

Love's Conduit

Each one of us is a piece within the majestic tapestry of life. You are an integral part of the whole, and the "whole" lives within you.

Take down your guard, lower your defenses, and open to all the love and joy that surrounds you.

When you try to control and manipulate, when you let fear and separation rule, you minimize the flow of love that abounds around us.

With each breath, in each moment, you can choose to be in harmony. Every smile you share sends ripples of love and acceptance.

Take time to listen and to see all the beauty abundantly and Divinely placed to sooth your soul. Open to the grace that sustains everyone and everything. Feel the warmth of the sun and the gentle light of the moon.

Allow love to move freely through every cell of your being. Feel its energy as it dances with you, through you, as you. Surrender your will to its majestic dance and ecstasy will dwell in your heart.

33

Make it a habit to look for the good and enjoy what is enjoyable in each moment.

Keep It Simple - Keep It Positive

I find it fascinating how much we like to complicate things! There is such a tendency to think that we can "improve" everything usually by adding some type of complexity to it.

The simple things of life are usually the most soul rewarding — Taking the time for a walk on the beach, holding hands with a loved one, sharing a smile with a stranger, slowing down enough to feel and enjoy the gentle caress of a summer breeze.

Look for what is beautiful in every moment and don't focus on "what could be better" …. See the love, joy and peace that sustains our existence and allow that to be your default focal point.

I have a good friend that I am sure is in my life to show me how not to relate to life. No matter what the situation is, he manages to find the one or two things that could be different and "better" in his eyes. Basically always finding life to be lacking, inadequate, unfair…

How many times do you find yourself being critical and unaccepting of people and situations? This is really a reflection of how much self-love and self-acceptance you have.

Know that we are all doing the best we can in a complicated world. Make it a habit to look for the good and enjoy what is enjoyable in each moment.

If you look for the beauty, your whole life will be surrounded by beauty. If you look to see love, your life will be love. What you seek will find you.

34

Your authentic self inherently flows in harmony with the Universe.

Be Your Authentic Self

You have to lose yourself to find Your-Self!

As a toddler your spirit is pure and fresh. All of your actions and interests are pure reflections of the Divine spirit within. Then all these outer restrictions and "teachings" start being imposed on you, and you start learning to shut down your "free spirit" energy. On top of that, you begin to absorb family and societal belief systems, and your authentic self gets buried under all those layers.

As you become older and want to become wiser, your job is to literally liberate that bright light within yourself. There is nothing new to learn, nothing else you need to acquire, or add to yourself. Your job is to start shedding all the layers that you have put on.

You see and interact with the world through the filters of intellect, beliefs, judgements, expectations, and your created personality identity with its inherent limitations.

It takes commitment and courage to start questioning everything you hold to be a truth, to look at the box from which you experience reality, and to step beyond that box. You must learn to see how you hold ourself back by the labels and expectations you place on ourself and others, and start living life with the power and freedom of the spirit within.

Your authentic self inherently flows in harmony with the Universe. Creativity and lightness are the fruits of that state. Self-acceptance and self- love is from where you function, because you have been set free from the shackles of fear and judgement.

Embrace the wholeness that you are by becoming naked. Live your life by following that inner knowing which wants to move like a salmon against the conventional current of knowledge and beliefs.

35

Trust the gentle whisper to lead you on your authentic path, to pave the way where there is no apparent road.

The Gentle Whisper

Listen for that gentle, loving voice from deep within. It holds all the wisdom of the Universe.

This caring voice is prodding you to follow your heart's desires, to express your Divine gifts as only you can, for the benefit of all mankind.

This beautiful voice is your North Star guiding you to your destiny. You cannot reach your personal peak by following the well-traveled road. That road just keeps you trapped in the fear and illusion of your small self.

Trust the gentle whisper to lead you on your authentic path, to pave the way where there is no apparent road.

This gentle whisper will get as strong as you let it be. It will take your fears away and fill you instead with love and joy as you fulfill your life's purpose.

Sit in silence, become intimate with yourself, follow the illogical path that leads to wisdom and liberation.

36

*Make the most out of every moment.
Your next experience will arrive in its own
perfect timing.*

Divine Timing

Divine timing is ever present, you just need to trust and listen for it. There is a rhythm and a pulse that runs through all creation. Every living thing abides by these except for humankind, who wants things to occur on their own separate time line.

Your desire to experience things immediately pulls you into not honoring or enjoying the process of growth and manifestation. It is not about the final outcome, it truly is about the journey.

A caterpillar only becomes a butterfly once it goes through its transformation. It needs to struggle in order to become strong enough to fly. You need a lifetime to become that truly beautiful person that is your potential. There is beauty and pain that you must experience. You go through heartache to learn how to love.

There are cycles, seasons, and stages in one's life. All arrive at the appropriate time. Your job is to fully engage in the moment that you are currently experiencing. Delve into what this moment is offering.

Are you alone? Explore it deeply. Are you raising small children? Make the most of it. Whatever is in your life right now, embrace it with all your energy. Don't try to rush through it or push it away because you just may miss what it is here to teach you, and you will have to repeat the lesson.

Nothing is permanent. Make the most out of every moment because it will never be repeated in quite the same way. Your next experience will arrive in its own perfect timing.

Learn to live life by your own inner rhythm. Take time to smell the roses, to play with the kids, to enjoy a deep conversation, to do the things that give you pleasure. Tomorrow will come in its own timing. Today belongs to you.

37

*Cultivate and follow your inner compass,
as it will never steer you wrong.*

Inner Knowing

Living an authentic life starts by developing and deepening your sense of inner knowing. You can cultivate your ability to hear and feel the energy and vibration of others, and clearly know whether this is a life-affirming connection for you or something to simply let move past you.

What people have called a "gut feeling," or intuition, is simply your ability to sense the energy around you and respond accordingly. The more intimate you are with yourself, the easier it is to recognize what belongs to you and what belongs to another.

No one is inherently right or wrong. It is a matter of whether their perspective aligns with your perspective. For example, are you both coming from a place of love and abundance or from a sense of fear and lack?

Learn to follow that very quiet whisper that lets you know there will be rough waters ahead if you start to deviate from your path. Feel and sense the world around you. It is always talking, informing you.

This world is full of carrots to entice you out of your deep knowing and integrity. There are many flashy toys and distractions pulling you out of your center. Cultivate and follow your inner compass, as it will never steer you wrong.

You know when you are in your highest truth by the total sense of well-being you are experiencing. Inner harmony creates outer harmony. Integrity within yourself creates integrity with others.

Wisdom arises from this place deep within you!

38

*See and experience life
from the deep calm waters of your soul.*

Dive Deep!

Be happy for the the life that you have, not the things that are in your life. Don't get caught up in all the shifting sand that comprises your life and stay in the awareness of this gift we call life.

There is an energy, a breath, a pulse, that brought you into existence and that keeps our bodies and the whole world alive. Open your heart and mind to it, and let it guide you through every experience that comes your way.

Dive deep within yourself and become one with this pulse. Get to know its love and joy. Rest in its peace and stillness. See and experience life from the deep calm waters of your soul.

39

*Stay true to yourself.
Enjoy the mystery inherent in the journey.*

Our Unfolding Lives

Our lives unfold in magical ways. There is a Divine plan for the intricate journey we call life. We must learn to sit back and enjoy the ride.

Our heart's longing inspires us to move in the best direction. Learn to see the unseen, to hear beyond the sounds, and to feel what is yet to come. Surrender to the mystery and savor each day as it comes.

Our lives unfold from the inside out. Start with baby steps and let life challenge and inspire you to grow from within. Maintain a grateful heart all along the journey. Each challenge is here to polish you and Grace is leading the way.

Don't let fear, and all its ugly cousins, get in your way. They are distortions and distractions that will block the light that dwells in your heart. Cultivate the qualities of love and you will be set free from the entanglements of life.

Each day you get to decide how to engage with the world. Choose love, look for the good, and see all that comes your way as the gift it actually is, unfolding for you to experience.

Stay true to yourself and enjoy the mystery inherent in the journey.

40

Set yourself free and express all your unique beauty.

Uniquely You

Acknowledge all that connects us and celebrate our differences. God is the ultimate artisan creating one of a kind pieces of art.

There is a spirit and energy that connects us to all there is, and this same energy expresses itself uniquely through you.

Allow this Holy Spirit within to dance and sing and celebrate each day as if it was its last one. No two snow flakes are the same, identical twins are externally similar, yet their spirits dance with their own rhythm and expression.

Don't let fear keep you small. Set yourself free and express all your unique beauty. We are not meant to be replicas of each other. We are here to add to the Divine quilt.

Follow your passion, allow your wildness to be expressed, share your beauty, and play with abandonment in the game of life!

41

*Love is the God energy.
Silence lets us be one with it.*

Love & Silence

Love and silence are the pillars of our path. Every step towards silence expands the love in our hearts. The love in our hearts pulls us into the silence of the present moment. It is a spiral we can ride into the center of our being.

As we move beyond our ego-centered experience and cultivate our unconditional love for the Divine, everything changes. Our life has meaning, our actions have integrity. Love creates our path.

Love is the God energy… Silence lets us be one with it.

42

*Be one with the empty space
that holds all possibilities.*

BE AN EMPTY VESSEL

Every day, take the time to empty yourself and create space for the Divine to fill you up. Empty yourself of earthly concerns and desires, open to something much more magnificent.

Most of us have minds overflowing with activity, like a broken record obsessing about insignificant things. You leave no room to receive your God-given inheritance of love and peace.

Stand naked each morning before putting on your ego, your external identity with its fears and desires. Be one with the empty space that holds all possibilities. Listen to the wisdom of the silence that lies within.

43

To know thy self is to become free!

Dedication and Practice

The yogic path is one of self-awareness. It is a daily journey into deeper levels of silence. Explore the silence inherent in all movement and the sounds in the depths of silence.

As you deepen the intimacy within yourself, you can sense your individual sound/vibration and that of those around you. You can feel the oneness with the universe, as well as your expression of that oneness living in you.

As a natural byproduct of your practice, peace and harmony rise to the surface. A calm mind will see the beauty that engulfs us. It can rest, feeling the energy that sustains us.

Moving from faith to direct experience of the Divine within, our small self releases and aligns to the greater universal energy. There is no struggle, no fear, only the calm joy inherent in deep peace.

It takes dedication and deep practice to explore all that lies below the surface of our being. To know thy self is to become free! It is a quantum shift that propels us into True awareness.

A top athlete breathes and lives his sport, and his dedication takes him to places others only dream about. A yogi needs this level of dedication to break through the limiting beliefs that keeps him small and bound. A burning desire, with total commitment for self-realization, shatters our sense of separation.

A yogi looks to know God and is not satisfied by knowing about Him… It is the direct experience that changes everything. Seeing the Divine in each flower, in each breath, in every moment, we bring heaven to earth.

44

*Following your path brings you into integrity,
it aligns your body, mind, and spirit in purpose and joy.*

Follow Your Passion

Inside each of us there is quiet desire to express ourselves in our unique way. Most of the time these desires do not easily fit with the expectations of everyday life.

Our true calling is usually accompanied by a feeling that it would be too hard, too risky, or maybe even impossible. What we don't realize is that the universe is here to guide and propel us to express and experience that which is living inside of us.

Our dreams and desires are meant to blossom in our lives. We must bring light to them and nurture them into maturity. We need to get out of our own way and bring our passion, intellect, and drive toward cultivating our hearts desires.

Are you thriving or just treading water? Is your life inspiring to you? When you get up are you excited about the day? If the answer is "no," then be aware that you are not living the life you were born to experience.

Shift direction, follow the inner compass of your heart, and rise to your potential. Following your path brings you into integrity, it aligns your body, mind, and spirit in purpose and joy.

There is never a perfect time or the perfect condition to get started but the minute you step into your passion, the path will be Divinely created for you.

45

*All love comes from within
as the direct expression of our Divine self.*

Being in Love

Something magical and transformative occurs as we allow love to dwell in us. Becoming an expression of love creates a blissful dance from deep within.

Being in love is sitting in the joy and stillness of connection. It is not an action, it is not agenda driven. It is a naked sharing of ourselves, an experience of oneness.

Love arises from a place of generosity. From fullness we share our bounty.

Love is a vibration that lives within us. It is a way of connecting with the world that sustains and surrounds us.

Love is light.

The seed of love, if cultivated, will grow into a magnificent tree that nurtures all who come in contact with its beauty and light.

All love comes from within as the direct expression of our Divine self. It is our ability to see that in ourselves, in others, and in the world that allows us to truly be in love.

46

Live life from the soul's perspective.

The Soul's Window

Our eyes are the windows of our soul. From within, we look to experience and express in this bountiful world.

Through the eyes of another we can see the mystery and depth we hold within ourselves, finite infinity dancing in space and time.

Through the eyes of our lover we enter the Divine stillness that completes us. We release and lose ourselves into that endless ocean that embraces us.

When the Divine in me recognizes the Divine in you, love becomes our abode. Harmony and beauty surrounds us, joy and laughter accompanies us.

Live life from the soul's perspective. Look out into the mystery contained in each moment while staying connected to the vast universe that lies within. Be the source, and the expression of that source, in this dance we call life.

47

Fully embrace, feel, and listen to what actually is.

LISTENING

In my writings and teachings, I place lots of emphasis on silence and stillness. It is my way of creating a space suitable to practice listening. We have both an outer world and an inner world in which we are in relationship.

Cultivating the ability to witness, to observe without an automatic reaction, is a powerful early step along our spiritual path. Observing the ebb and flow of our minds and allowing for the shifting sands of life are critical for inner peace and contentment.

To fully listen, our ego-self must get out of the way. In order to listen for the sake of understanding we must not be thinking of our position on the matter (not thinking about what we will say next). Letting go of our agenda around the subject is how we can fully embrace, feel and listen to what actually is.

Our minds have been programed by our past experiences and everything that they perceive is interpreted by those programs. With practice, we go beyond the programs to have a clean perception of reality.

48

If you stop all activity and start witnessing the moment, a rush of aliveness arises.

The Lost Art of Non-Doing

Our ego-selves needs to be constantly engaging with the world. They are fed by the things we do, by the activities that define our own identities. Notice how many times you reach out to check your phone, look at Facebook and check emails. When you do have some free time, do you fill it up with activity?

The ego knows itself in relation to others, to the outer world. It knows itself within polarity, in contrast to what it perceives. Our ego is what makes us feel separate from all there is.

If you stop all activity and start witnessing the moment, a rush of aliveness arises. An interconnectedness and a sense of oneness appears as we let go of our need to differentiate ourselves.

There is an art to allowing, to simply being in the moment for the joy inherent in it. Leaving "ourselves" out of the moment and fully opening to what is occurring, takes us into a whole new awareness beyond our limiting beliefs.

49

*Letting go of all that differentiates us
and nakedly opening to what is in the present moment,
is how we discover our limitless selves.*

Liberation

There is a multi-step process in cultivating freedom. We are born as a blank slate. As we start having experiences, our minds create a story about all that has occurred. These stories become the programs from which we interpret all that comes our way, and the stories are that which we project into our potential future.

These experiences are held deep within our cellular structures. They are our unconscious clingings to the past, which impedes our true freedom. We are like a garden full of weeds that interfere with the growth of the beautiful flowers we are looking to cultivate.

In meditation practice we are taught to cultivate the witness state. We observe our thoughts and emotions, develop perspective, and create some freedom since we are not automatically reacting to every situation. I see this stage as maturing our ego, developing some wisdom. We have removed some of the larger weeds from the garden.

This witness state still belongs to the ego, it still contains the trappings of our beliefs and limitations. Our Divine self is beyond this state. It is an egoless state of being-ness.

In releasing our self-image, letting go of all that differentiates us and nakedly opening to what is in the present moment, is how we discover our limitless selves. Shedding our layers in contemplation and meditation gives us glimpses of this reality beyond the veil of polarity.

It is a place of direct experience. There is no filtering, interpreting, or judging based on our ego perspective.

50

*Aligning our hearts and minds to the greater energy that lives within us,
allows us to effortlessly navigate and experience the life before us.*

Be Centered

All of our efforts should be directed at staying centered in ourselves and connected to the Divine energy that dwells within us. Holding this state of awareness is what allows us to live a life full of love and joy.

If we spend our days looking to control our outer world, there will always be the feelings of effort and survival. Our energies will get depleted and our minds will be anxious.

By finding first and then sustaining this inner peace and harmony, we are in a place of receiving and enjoying the day that is gifted to us. This is a major paradigm shift that will change our whole reality.

In our physical yoga practice, we use our muscle energy to hug our midline and to skillfully align our skeletal system. Once we are in our optimal alignment, our body has much more strength and flexibility allowing our poses to be expressed with very little effort and a feeling of joy easily flows from within.

In the same manner, aligning our hearts and minds to the greater energy that lives within us, allows us to effortlessly navigate and experience the life before us.

Our ego thinks it is separate and it needs to control things. Our heart knows our oneness and softens to receive the gifts of the day. We have the power to balance these energies in a way that makes our days meaningful and enjoyable.

Before you get up in the morning, take the time to connect with your stilled center. Open to the Divine that dwells in you and let it guide you through the day.

51

*That magical place when all that you are,
is in one moment of time and space.*

Yoga is a State of Being

It is that magical place when all that we are, is in one moment of time and space. When our mind, body, and soul are fully present and harmoniously integrated, we are in the Yogic state.

There are many tools we can use to help us create this state. But those tools are not Yoga. This state may be achieved without any of the traditional practices that people call yoga.

It is important to differentiate the actions that lead us to a certain state of being, and the actual being state of integration and liberation that is Yoga.

In our lives there will be times when circumstances come together in such a way that we enter this joyous and alive place by pure Grace. It comes from a place of letting go. Not really from what we actually do.

Most of the yoga and meditation training is to learn how to actively open and surrender into a space where this state can be experienced. It is always within us, but we place barriers that block us from being there.

Our ego-mind gives us a false sense of separateness and this leads into feelings of fear, lack, and the need to control. The Yogic being state is blocked when we are in our small ego mind.

52

Freedom is the fruit of our spiritual work.

Emotions are Reflections of Attachments

Emotions are a good way to determine to what extent we are functioning from our ego personality state. Our emotions show our need to "control" the outer circumstances of our lives. Are we grasping, pulling, pushing things to go the way we would like things to be? Do we get upset because someone is not behaving in the way we want them to? Do we feel something lacking in us that must be acquired externally?

The way we feel, the emotions that are our "baseline," is the vibration from which we relate to the world and from where we co-create. Happiness and sadness are how we feel around certain situations, but joy is an internal state.

As we move deeper into our center, we develop an inner sense of joy, peace, and stillness that become our base vibration. We respond to the changing world without reacting from fear-based emotions.

As long as we feel that our well-being comes from outside ourselves, we will be scheming, manipulating, and trying to control those around us. Anger, frustration, stress, and fear will be the baseline emotions and the vibration from which life is being lived.

By cultivating a deep connection to the light within, we become free of the lower, negative vibrations of life. By being in direct and intimate relationship with the source that creates the Universes, we are able to relax and enjoy the ebb and flow that is part of the human experience.

When challenging situations come our way, we are able to be loving and compassionate to others. There is empathy and understanding of other's perspectives and actions. We will also have the freedom of choosing how we would like to respond to what is occurring based on the level of witness consciousness and detachment that has been acquired.

Freedom is the fruit of our spiritual work. Freedom to be able to walk away from any situation, to honor our truths and live in our integrity, to love and live life in all its glory and potential… Freedom to be you!

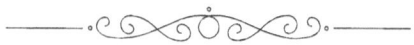

53

Doing what you love just for the sake of doing it, is our grandest expression.

BEING ORDINARY

Being ordinary is the most extraordinary way to be. Simply being yourself is the grandest version of your being.

Expressing all the facets of you in an open and vulnerable way is your most powerful gift to the Universe. Embracing your uniqueness and sharing as much of your God-given light is how you live your purpose and fulfill your dharma.

Don't be afraid of your magnificence. Don't chase the glory. Simply express what lives within you for its own sake, no fear and no glory, just because it needs to be expressed.

The ego is looking for recognition and avoiding being seen as a failure. Inherently, this situation distorts your natural expression. Yet, doing what you love just for the sake of doing it, is your grandest expression.

It is futile to compare ourself with others with your outer accomplishments. The real prize is how authentic you can be, how much of your light is expressed in you, how much joy and passion do you experience each day, each moment.

An authentic you is much more valuable than living a life chasing an outer expression of a society defined "successful you". The quality of your being is the yardstick from which to live. Choose love, peace and joy. Be in harmony with yourself and others.

54

We are not victims of our circumstances.

It's Our Choice

There is an energy that gives us life, that pulsates inside of us and that is always expressing itself through us. It keeps the ebb and flow of our breath, feeds our imagination, brings longing to our hearts.

This energy has the freedom to express the full spectrum of the human condition; love, fear, hate, compassion, division, and oneness. We are the ones that can cultivate and channel the expression that we bring to our lives, to our world.

It is our privilege and responsibility to work with this Divine energy to shape and mold the life we are living. We are not victims of our circumstances. We are powerful beyond our imaginations and we are more than capable of channeling and managing this life force within.

The world can challenge us with its polarity and its endless possibilities. It invites us to look deep within to that reservoir of pure Divine love for guidance.

We have the freedom to express the whole range of "good and evil, light or dark." We need to know ourselves and actively choose in each moment to be the best version of ourselves.

Make the choice to listen, to be generous and kind, to smile, to be compassionate, to love….In each moment we can choose the higher path!

Be mindful and aware of all that we are and choose to be a light in our human fabric.

55

Nothing here remains forever.

Passing Through

We are in this world but not of this world. We are journeying through space and time, taking on roles and personalities as we play with one another. Its all a game, all a play. Nothing here remains forever.

Savor this precious time on Mother Earth with all her gifts and beauty. Live each day awakened in truth and freedom. Choose to be love and light. Dance, sing, and express yourself. Play with abandonment and bring joy all around you.

Be authentically you in every moment. Don't let fear keep you small. Don't let society define your role or worth. Dance and express the truth that is in your heart and when your time is done there will be no regrets.

It is not about big accomplishments nor great external success. It is about the love, light, and joy that you can carry within yourself and share with the world. Each role is equally important. Be authentically and fully you!

56

*Why chase shadows when you can
live in the splendor of the light?*

There is Only One Answer

God is the only solution for all of our problems. Trying to fix every single issue one at a time is a misguided way of living our lives. We are tangled up micromanaging things at the lower vibration, which allows those issues to exist and to thrive in the first place.

By placing our efforts to connecting to the universal force that is life itself, all things come into proper balance. Basically, we don't have to understand the darkness, just bring the light to it.

We can psychoanalyze ourselves forever and we will be stuck in the realm of our ego-self trying to make sense of a false reality but if we shift our whole perspective by our direct connection to the Divine within, the whole paradigm shifts. A new reality comes into existence.

The light removes our fundamental fear, lack consciousness, and separation misperception. We get to experience the love and security of being connected to source.

Every single day, make it your priority to be in communion with your higher self. Rest in its power and light. Surrender to the ebb and flow of existence and open to the Joy that lives within you.

Why chase shadows when you can live in the splendor of the light?

57

*Unbound creative energy expressed from a place of
freedom and lightness of being,
is our birth right and our full potential.*

Creating Freedom

Yoga is about creating freedom in our beings. Becoming unbound in our physical bodies, mental bodies, emotional bodies and energetic bodies; systematically releasing the physical and mental, conscious and subconscious patterns and beliefs that keep us trapped in unhealthy bodies, unhealthy relationships, unhappy lives.

There is an optimal way to being in alignment with the Universal energy and misalignments can be seen in our physical bodies, mental attitudes, levels of happiness, and satisfaction with our lives. By consistently and methodically choosing to be in optimal alignment, we can profoundly change the quality of our lives.

There is an optimal skeletal and muscular structure to our bodies which allows for full range of motion, stability, strength, poise and grace. Through intelligent asana practice, we can therapeutically retrain our physical bodies to move to their optimal states. These optimal physical states allow energy to fully flow, which brings us to our natural states of health and well-being.

Our physical bodies hold on to stress and negative emotions by becoming tight and rigid. We literally lose the freedom to move and respond in an open and full way. We have built these restrictions through a lifetime of living and facing the challenges that life brings our way.

As yogis, from a place of knowledge and safety, we move to change our patterns. We open our physical bodies through asana practice. We expand our energy bodies through breath work, we expand our framework of beliefs by studying yogic philosophy and we develop direct experience of our divine selves through meditation.

Yoga offers a well lit path to move from pain, fear, anxiety and emptiness to optimal health, and a sense of inner joy and contentment. How far we move along this spectrum is directly related to our levels of desire and dedication to our own evolvement and transformation. There is a huge difference from doing yoga to becoming a yogi. It is a way of being in life that transports us to a whole new reality.

Cultivating higher levels of freedom in our own being allows our most profound light to be expressed. Unbound creative energy expressed from a place of freedom and lightness of being, is our birth right and our full potential.

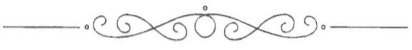

58

By becoming more intimate with yourself each day, and by embracing all facets of your being, you acquire the wisdom and knowledge to create a life worth living.

Navigating Life

Imagine yourself as the captain of your own sailboat. You will spend your whole life on that vessel, and it can take you anywhere you can skillfully navigate. The only limitations you have are those you impose on yourself.

I am talking about cultivating a state of "being" that is always looking to be in harmony with the reality you are experiencing. I see it as being a master sailor of your own life. You have your ship, you have the freedom to choose the destinations. What limits you is your knowledge.

Do you understand the stars that guide us? Can you plan accordingly for the long haul? Have you developed the mental and physical strength for the journey you are choosing to make? Are you flexible and patient enough to move in harmony with nature, with life?

We all begin life in the same way and we all have the same final destination. In between these two points you have the opportunity to express your own unique light. Fears, un-healthy habits and hidden patterns in yourself are the challenges that life places before you to make the journey more worthwhile. These challenges hide you from your own divinity, blocking you from experiencing your own true nature.

There is an inner compass, a wisdom, to be cultivated. It will take you on your individual journey towards the greatest expression of yourself.

By choosing everyday to remember who you are, by honoring the wisdom inherent in each moment, by becoming more intimate with yourself each day, and by embracing all facets of your being, you acquire the wisdom and knowledge to create a life worth living. Not one driven by lack and fear but one full of love, understanding, and respect.

59

*Actively engage in every moment
and its richness will be revealed to you.*

Flowing with the Natural Cycles

There is a very simple cycle to all of existence. There is a beginning, a middle and an end. We create, sustain and dissolve. It is simply energy moving from one stage to the next and the next.

There is a natural ease and flow. Winter, spring, summer and fall are all equal manifestations of Divine expression. It is the same energy uniquely expressed.

Everything that is in existence is deteriorating, while simultaneously there is always a rebirth happening. Every seven years, all of the cells in our bodies have been replaced.

Learning to fully engage with where we are in every moment allows us to fully enjoy and engage the life we are living. We perceive some things as being more effort than others, but that is a game of the mind. If we live the day with presence, it would be the same effort to go to the beach than to do office work, but our mind associates one with pleasure and the other with responsibility.

Each day has an expression desiring to blossom. Skillfully embrace what is here today and then let it go, so that you can fully be with the next moment, the next expression. Actively engage in every moment and its richness will be revealed to you.

The sensation of effort gets created when we choose not to be in the natural flow, when we choose to see the activity as something imposed on us. It is based on our relationship to what is actually occurring.

Learn to flow like water, effortlessly moving to fill up and experience all that is on its path.

60

*If we listen to the gentle whisper of our soul
we will be Divinely guided every second of our lives.*

Divine Guidance

There is an outer knowing and an inner wisdom. There is a logical, society acceptable, externally driven path to our lives and an inner guided, heart driven, individualized path we can choose. One leads us to an authentic expression of ourselves, and the other challenges us with a disintegration of our being.

If we listen to the gentle whisper of our soul we will be Divinely guided every second of our lives. This guidance always points to our highest potential and challenges us to move beyond our fears and limiting beliefs, taking us to a place of true freedom and empowerment.

This inner knowing is our Buddha self, our inner guru. It is the light within that leads us along our unique, uncharted path towards fulfillment and liberation. It takes courage and dedication to cultivate the integration of an external life guided by our internal knowing.

Our practices lead us to direct experiences of our inner world. From the gentle movement of energy, to having feelings of wholeness and safety, to literally seeing other realities with our inner eyes. The more we develop our connection to our deeper self, the easier it becomes to follow its gentle guidance.

Once this light has been opened in us, we are no longer blind. Once we feel this energy, we are no longer alone. We are transformed from within into our highest expressions.

61

*Opening to the Divine,
is allowing light to come into your life.
Your path and purpose will be well-lit.
Harmony and integrity will be your natural state.*

God Consciousness

For those of us on the Path, our goal is to have experiences that allow our ego-mind to have a direct knowledge of our Divine self. Spiritual practices are designed to lead us into this personal connection with the Divine within.

God consciousness is nothing more than having a knowledge, an awareness of the Divine, of God. Once we have this awareness, we see the blessings and God's hand in everything around us. We can release our struggles and open to the Grace that supports us in every moment.

By quieting the mind, we can soften into the wisdom of the present moment. It is here that we can experience the subtle peace and joy of our deeper self. Cultivating this inner state allows us to know the harmony and beauty that surrounds us.

If our ego mind only knows itself as a separate being, it will stay in a state of fear and lack. It will be aggressive, protective, apathetic, and will have a deep sense of dissatisfaction with life. This is truly the lost Garden of Eden.

We need to move from a philosophical understanding of God to a direct experience of this magnificent force that lives as us and is the whole Universe.

Without this connection, we are exiled to a life in darkness. There is no real purpose, no clear path. Opening to the Divine, is allowing light to come into our lives. Our path and purpose will be well-lit. Harmony and integrity will be our natural state.

62

*Align to God, let grace guide you
and your wildest aspirations will unfold before you…
Let magic be a daily occurrence.*

Magic Happens!

As we begin to travel in awareness and connection to the force that sustains the Universe, we can see magic all around us. The miracle of life can be experienced in every moment, if we choose to see it.

Our own ignorance closes the curtain that keeps the light out of our existence. We must make the conscious choice to open the blinds and let in the magic and beauty that surrounds us.

This light is always looking for a crack to let its rays in and guide us back into its splendor and joy. I asked a friend, who had had a major drinking problem, how he ended up getting sober and he answered "I don't know, I was all screwed up when it happened."

He let in just enough light to bring him back from the abyss he was living. He did not have to figure it out. He allowed the magic to live in him. Two years after not having a drink, he realized that he was actually sober.

The more we actively express the light that lives in us, the greater the opening we create for magic to direct and shape the life around us.

Align to God, let grace guide you and your wildest aspirations will unfold before you… Let magic be a daily occurrence.

63

*Let go and dance with abandonment
in this journey of time and space.*

Let Spirit have its Way with You

Become an empty vessel and allow Spirit to have its way with you.

Make the Divine your lover and lose yourself in the ecstasy of love. Forget your name, and release your fears and boundaries. Open to the joy and bliss living inside of you.

The drop releases into the ocean and it finds its true essence. Let go and dance with abandonment in this journey of time and space.

Let peace, love, and Joy have their way with you today!

64

*Break out from your own imposed chains
by bringing awareness and light to your inner universe.*

Personal Revolution

We need to embark on a personal revolution to reclaim our innate freedom. We have the ability to be happy and to follow our greatest desires, and yet many of us feel trapped in the life we are living.

It is our birth right to love as we want to love, to express our unique light, and to live the life we were born to experience. Yet, our ego-self constrained by society's norms and our own imposed limitations block us from within.

Break out from your own imposed chains by bringing awareness and light to your inner universe. Embrace your Divine light as it will free you from your shadows and distortions.

Your small ego-self can become a tyrant. It lives within the distortions of polarity. It feeds on fear, lack, and separation and enslaves you in the mirage of life. Your higher self, the light within, has the power to set you free and to bring the ego to its rightful place as your servant, helping you to co-create the highest expression of your life.

The spiritual path leads you into a Divine revolution. You start to see the bullshit around you and you stop tolerating the lower vibrations that keep you trapped. It is a path toward the light that brings out your greatest gifts.

It is a revolution because you are transformed, you are set free to fly and soar into unknown territory. Fear and separation are slain so that love can reign in your own garden of Eden.

65

*Cultivate daily silence and stillness,
and the light will reveal itself.
It is there already waiting for you to see it.*

Look Within

All of our mystics and master teachers have taught us to look within. They were all rebels in their lifetimes, usually going against the established religions which had moved away from their original teachings.

Religions are created by the followers of the master. From their perspective they create rules and codes of conduct to try and duplicate what they witnessed. The teachings became polluted by the "humanness" of its leaders. With time, it became driven by power and control, and full of all the trappings of the life that they were meant to liberate us from. Fear, lack, and separation are the hallmarks of religion.

The call of our times is to become masters ourselves. To be transformed by our practices and be directly connected to the Divine that dwells in us.

There is a Holy Spirit that will guide us home. Our job is to shift our focus from outer distractions toward our inner being. Cultivate daily silence and stillness, and the light will reveal itself. It is there already waiting for you to see.

66

*We are the Earth Angels,
the answer to other's prayers.*

We Are It

We are the Earth Angels, the answer to other's prayers. Here on Earth we are the manifest-ors and the carriers of the light. It is up to us to make a better world by every word, expression, and action we take.

Big gestures matter and are important, such as when the wealthy create foundations to do humanitarian work. It is wonderful that they want to share their bounty and help society in a way that they can.

But we must remember that their work is equal to the effort we make when we take the time to listen and support those around us. As important as a smile freely shared, support given, an open heart.

We can make anyone's day by simply being present. Seeing them with love and compassionate understanding.

By cultivating love and joy in our hearts, we become the light that supports others. It is really so simple.

A kinder, gentler society is created by each of us taking the time to touch someone's heart everyday. It creates a ripple effect that moves all of us into higher vibrations.

Prayers need to be answered by one of us. We are the ones that facilitate for one another. We need to extend a helping hand. We are the angels working in the manifested world.

You have the power to positively impact every single person that you encounter today. Shine your light as brightly as you can and become a tsunami of love and joy in your neck of the woods.

67

Any dis-ease that we experience is simply letting us know that there are misalignments with how we are relating to life. It is a call to purify and to align to the higher energy of love and joy, our natural state.

Perfect Health is our Natural State

Self healing is achieved by coming into our optimal alignment physically, mentally, and emotionally. We are multi faceted beings and each of our bodies affects and influences the other.

Our thoughts affect our mood which is also reflected in our bodies - (physical, emotional, mental & energetic). There is a feed back loop with each being influenced and being an influencer for the other.

We can efficiently find balance by playing with this interconnectedness. For example, when you are feeling stressed and you go for a run or a yoga class, you will change your mood and calm your system. Notice how a small physical injury will negatively affect your mood and also shift how the rest of the body feels.

As yogis we learn physical, mental, and breath (energy) practices which look to bring our whole system into its optimal state of functioning. Making it a daily habit of performing these practices is a key to our well-being.

When we achieve optimal muscle balance around our skeletal system our bodies become pain free and our life force flows with no friction. As we learn to calm our minds, the stress in our lives is diminished and we live with clarity and purpose.

In daily living we are constantly digesting food and experiences and that comes with a certain level of challenge and toxicity. These practices help us purify our being and digest all that comes our way.

Any dis-ease that we experience is simply letting us know that there are misalignments with how we are relating to life. It is a call to purify and to align to the higher energy of love and joy, our natural state.

68

Make the inner journey of transmutation and transformation that brings you into alignment with your highest purpose.

Situations Will Not Change Until You Change

Our outer world is a reflection of what is going on within ourselves. It is an outer expression of the inner workings of our being.

Each of us lives in our own universe of beliefs and conditioning. We have blinders that only allow us to perceive a narrow range of life, based on those inner restrictions. We live in our own reality box! The only way to make powerful changes in our lives is by becoming free and expanding out of that box. We must transform our inner being.

We suppress feelings, fears and desires. We feel criticized and judged by others. There is a tension inside all of us from not being able to fully live in the manner we would like. These energies distort reality and create the life we are living.

Also, inside ourselves, is the light of awakening. We hold our own salvation. By working directly with our own being, we can change all of reality. We can spend less time looking outwards and direct our attention to becoming our best selves. Taking one small step at a time, we can find the light that is uniquely our own.

The yoga path requires us to accept responsibility. It is a mature path that acknowledges that it is up to us to make the inner journey of transmutation and transformation that brings us into alignment with our highest purpose.

There is no room for blaming others or playing victim to our circumstances because we understand that all these challenges are here for our growth and evolution. We have the gift of free will and therefore we are responsible for the choices we make. Always make the highest choice. Become the light and love you want to see in the world.

69

*To welcome the new,
the old must be released.*

Travel Light

Life is only lived in the present moment. We must actively shed the old that is no longer needed and make room for the new to be expressed.

Nothing holds us back as much as our outdated patterns of who we used to be. They creep up in the strangest places to sabotage our journey forward.

Every moment offers a new beginning, pregnant with unlimited potential. The only things that blocks us from manifesting our highest self are the old patterns that we continue to hold on to. We remain stuck in how things used to be or attached to an illusion of a reality that never existed. These old patterns are attached to us through the energy of fear.

Our spiritual path requires us to become naked and sober. We can leave the past behind and truly see the gifts that await us in the experience of an awakened life.

How many of us are, or have been stuck in relationships that are no longer life affirming, jobs that no longer fulfill us? Have we felt trapped in the life we are living? These feelings are a call to action!

In no way am I implying to throw the baby out with the bath water. I am saying that we must allow changes to come into us and renegotiate those things that are no longer valid. Some will be left behind and others will be transformed to fit the new self.

The changes come from within and they ripple out into our lives. To welcome the new, the old must be released.

70

*Make love with the Divine,
in the here and now.*

Life, Our Lover

Let the beauty of each moment pull on your heart and draw you into the joy of living.

The mind races from the past into the future but life exists in the present.

Life, is our greatest lover. She seduces us with all her beauty and gifts. Sunrises and sunsets, flowers and birds, delights to our senses. Stop and savor all she freely offers to fill our hearts with love and joy.

God created this paradise for us to frolic in like innocent children. See, listen, taste, and touch the world that has been gifted to us.

The seasons dance around us, the sun and moon play hide and seek above us. Don't waste your time in the shadows and fears of your mind. Make love with the Divine, in the here and now.

71

*It's the journey,
not the destination.*

Becoming

There is a lot of talk about and focus on the law of attraction and how it will bring to you all these wonderful things and people that will make you happy.

This line of thinking takes you away from the perfection of the present moment and has you focused on what is missing now by projecting your energy into the future.

Its not about the outward manifestation, but the inner experience of becoming. It's the journey, not the destination.

As I am writing, I am truly enjoying the experience of putting into words the teachings that live inside of me. I am not writing with the focus of the final product of this book. That may arrive in a future moment of time. In the here and now, I am fully in the process of exploring these topics that are of importance to me and I am enjoying my evolution into becoming an author.

Channel your energy into becoming the person that you want to be. It is always an inside job. As you mature and arrive at the best expression of yourself, your outer world will have all of its fruits and blossoms.

Living and striving for outer goals will leave you empty and unfulfilled. Becoming your highest self will bring levels of well being beyond your greatest expectations.

If you are driven by lack or fear your whole experience will be tainted. But, if you are driven by the love to explore and share the passion and desires you are looking to embody within yourself, there will be a fundamental joy and contentment inside of you.

It is not about writing a book, it is about experiencing the process of becoming an author.

72

Follow your bliss and surrender to the process that will bring you from a seed to a majestic expression of your innate potential.

The Fire of Transformation

Embrace the journey and surrender to the fire within that shapes you like a work of art. Allow the fire of life to mold and shape you into the highest version of yourself.

Follow your bliss and surrender to the process that will bring you from a seed to a majestic expression of your innate potential.

All of the universe conspires to draw out the most refined and purified versions of yourself. That process is usually quite intense in order to create the necessary pressure for a quantum shift in your being. You need to let go of all you think you are, so that you can blossom into a much higher version of yourself.

Don't fight back or try to run away. Surrender and allow this Divine fire to have its way with you and draw out all of your beauty and grace!

73

*Love never ends,
it simply changes form.
Love has always, and will always, be!*

Love Is All There Is

The whole Universe comes from the love and breath of the Divine. There is simply nothing else!

Anything less than unconditional love is the shadow cast on this magnificent light. The light is not diminished in any way, it is simply not flowing in its full spectrum.

The Sun is always sending us its light and warmth. Clouds getting in the way does not diminish the sun rays nor the Sun itself. We are the ones that manage the clouds in our lives.

Our work is to minimize and remove all obstacles that block the light. By our spiritual practices we purify our body and mind so that we can carry and reflect the Divine within in its most pure form.

In this game of free will, we can choose to carry the lower expressions of this fundamental light. We have the freedom to create clouds all around us. Out of the energy of love, we can choose to express fear, hate, and lack. We can also choose not to see the light/love that is right in front of us and that lives in us.

There is no higher calling than to open to the light. Embody and express the love that is our fundamental energy. It is the only thing that is real in this plane of time and space.

Love never ends, it simply changes form. Love has always, and will always, be!

74

Hold the mirror of love and acceptance.

Holding the Mirror

As a spiritual teacher, all I can do is to remind you of the truth that lives inside of you. My words resonate with your inner wisdom, and there is a remembrance of the magic that is you.

We have so many layers of false beliefs surrounding our inner truthes. It is like peeling an onion to connect to the light that lies at our core. As teachers all we can do is reflect the light of you, so that you can wake up from the ego dream state.

Our children are amazing mirrors of the false self from which we live. Their simple and sometimes annoying questions always point out the outer programming of fear and control that runs through our lives.

Notice how we want to push and mold our children into conforming to societal expectations. Notice our need to "help" them become more "successful" in their lives.

At an early age there is the wisdom that we just want to be happy, that we want to express something uniquely ours. We just want to be loved and accepted for who we are. This is the greatest gift we can still give to one another.

Some of us are more intellectual, others, street smart, introverts and extroverts, tall and short. Each of us brings something unique and special to the world we share. Become the light that is cultivated through self love and self acceptance. See the beauty in all of our unique expressions. Hold the mirror of love and acceptance.

Fear and lack are only perceived from an inauthentic place. If you are freely living the passion that dwells in you there will rise a contentment and a knowing that nothing is missing in you. All your thoughts and actions will come from a place of love and abundance.

75

Dance your dance!

Follow the Rhythm

Attune to the music that resides in your heart and dance your dance! Live in the trance of your own inner drummer, let its rhythm move your body and soothe your soul.

Don't overthink, don't let fear hold you back. Listen for the beat and the rhythm that will guide you along the way. Become intoxicated in its ecstasy and let lightness and freedom make their way with you.

Open to the joy of expressing your own inner dance, trust its Divine guidance. It is love looking to express itself through you, as you.

76

Beliefs and actions keep us bound.

Thoughts and Karma

Karma is expressed in the actions we take, and our actions are dictated by the thoughts and beliefs we hold. Based on the interconnectedness of cause and effect, we can see how thoughts, beliefs and actions keep us bound in the life we are living.

We have the power to change and direct our Karma. It requires developing awareness and control of our thoughts and actions. It demands that we take responsibility for who we are in the world and steadily change how we think, relate to, and act in our lives.

We live our lives on automatic pilot. Each day blends into the next without the deep questions. We have given up control of our lives feeling trapped in the existence we have created. Our lives has a most probable outcome based on the projection of our travels due to our "karma" (our thoughts and actions).

Wake up to the knowledge that you can take control of your future by consciously changing your thoughts and actions. What you are living and experiencing now was created by the beliefs you had in the past. Your future will be determined by your thoughts and actions in the present moment. You can go on recreating the past or create something new.

Expand your thinking and start taking small steps toward the life you would like to experience. The whole universe will conspire to manifest your consistent thoughts and actions. You are the architect of your life. Create your dreams by consciously using the law of Karma through active control of your thoughts, believes, and actions.

Don't let fear hold you back from your innate potential. Small steps toward your dreams are all that is required.

77

*The passion in our hearts
is the compass for our lives.
Above all else, be true to yourself.*

What Turns You On?

What brings you joy? Where do you go to when left to your own devices? What soothes your soul? What nurtures you from deep within?

These are windows into your innate nature. Here lies your strength and potential waiting to be developed and explored. Immerse yourself in what pulls the strings of your heart.

We tend to focus on what is missing, on what our weaknesses are, as we compare ourselves to the strengths in others. Yet, if we fully engage in our passion it will lead us on our unique path; the path that we came prepared to walk, that will pull on our strengths and that will draw out our gifts.

The passion in our hearts is the compass for our lives. It leads us into our life purpose, our dharma. It won't necessarily be an easy path, but it will be our authentic path. With practice and dedication, we will bring to the light the potential waiting to be expressed.

Don't follow anyone else's path. Others are successful and happy because they are living their own truths. You can learn from them and enjoy their bright and authentic light, but follow your own inner counsel.

You are never wrong about your dreams and desires. It does take skill and patience to cultivate what is wanting to be expressed through you, as you. You must remain steady amidst all the fear and shadows that appear to be blocking your path. In reality, they are there to help you adjust your path for a more direct route to your destination.

Above all else, be true to yourself. Take courage sitting in your stillness and trust the creative energy expressing itself through you.

78

*Come from a place of abundance and
share the joy that is in your heart.
It will create the life you were born to experience.*

Live in Love & Joy!

Once you remove the fear from your life, all that is left is love and joy. See what you have piled on yourself that is creating stress and tension in your life, and make the changes that will make your spirit free and happy.

You are not in charge, God is…Your only responsibility is to be open to the love and light that dwells within you.

Worrying and trying to control your uncertain future diminishes your love and light. It shrivels your creative powers. It makes you small and weak.

Come from a place of abundance and share the joy that is in your heart. It will create the life you were born to experience.

Learn to move and live in harmony with the here and now. Open yourself to the blessings that are accompanying you right now. Everyday do something that brings you joy. Rest in the love of the Great Spirit that is and sustains all of existence.

79

Each one of us is an integral part of the whole of existence, and we exist as a unique tapestry in the universal quilt.

Oneness Consciousness

The highest state of our yogic path is arriving at the awareness that we are all one. Each one of us is an integral part of the whole of existence, and we exist as a unique tapestry in the universal quilt.

We are all interconnected as we share a common consciousness. Our ego/personality perspective creates the illusion of separation and all of the emotions of lack and fear.

When we gaze into the eyes of another we can glance at the soul that unites us. When we open our hearts to the human condition, love and compassion spring forth from within.

We are all created from the same source energy and we all return to the same place. Here, we are nothing more than individual rays of the one true sun.

Our path requires us to break away from the grip of our ego so that we can directly experience the totality that unites us. We must lose ourselves to find our essence.

Attachments to our identity and our possessions bind us to the ego reality. Opening to our inner universe through meditation and devotional practices unbinds us from our false reality.

As humans we have the free will to remain enslaved in our own delusions or to awaken to the light and truth that lies within.

80

As light beings we need to maintain practices that purify and clean out all that blocks our light. Underneath these layers of "dirt", what exists is the pure fragrance of Love.

Spiritual Bathing

Our spiritual practices are meant to clean and purify our being from all the physical, mental, and emotional toxins that we take in from daily living.

Imagine how you would feel if you had not showered in a couple of days, a week, a month. You would be pretty "stinky". How much grime would be stuck to you and how unpleasant would you be to others.

As light beings we need to maintain practices that purify and clean out all that blocks our light. Underneath these layers of "dirt", what exists is the pure fragrance of Love.

Notice how good you feel after a nice long shower. You become refreshed and renewed. That is nothing in comparison to cleaning out all the unhealthy energy that is weighting you down and distorting your perception of the light and beauty that surrounds you, and is you.

Spiritual practice needs to become part of your daily routine, just as brushing your teeth and taking a shower. If done daily, your well-being will be easily maintained and joy and love will accompany you through out your days.

81

*Bring your attention
to the goodness that surrounds you.
Move toward peace, joy, and love.*

What Are You Nourishing?

My grandfather was a cattle farmer in central Cuba. He loved his farm and his cattle. While he had men that worked the farm for him, he made the point of being there everyday. One of his favorite phrases was that the cattle were nourished more by his love and attention than by the food they were eating.

My grandfather always wore an easy smile. He had the peace and love of a great sage, cultivated thought his faith, his love for family and the land. He passed away when I was 6 years old and yet I can clearly feel his presence in the man I have become.

A plague attacked his cattle and for several months one or two of his cows were dying weekly and no one knew what to do. He stayed calm and in faith, saying that the only reason he could lose them was because he had been blessed by having them in the first place. He weathered the storm with the peace he had cultivated within himself. Loving his blessings but not becoming attached to them. Understanding the ebb and flow that is life.

I learned from him that what we place value on and nourish with our attention will come to fruition. Don't waste your life pursuing things, glory, or fame. These are all shadows and temptations from our separate ego self.

Don't focus on your fears nor the things you perceive lacking in you. Bring your attention to the goodness that surrounds you. Move toward peace, joy, and love.

Cultivate the quality of your being. Expand your capacity for love. Connect to the source that creates and sustains the Universe. Know the light that lives inside of you.

82

*That which you seek
is hiding in plain sight.*

STOP SEEKING

Stop seeking God for he is right here, all around you, in you as you. That which you seek is hiding in plain sight. Stop, be silent, feel him in each breath, in the warmth and the cold, in the sun and the moon. Anywhere you look he is there. All you need to do is shift your perception and be still.

For many years, I defined myself as a seeker of God, of Divine truth. I spent endless hours looking for the next spiritually high experience. Until one day, I realized that if I was always seeking I could never simply be one with the Divine. It was the same ego game of not being satisfied and always looking for more.

That's when I decided to no longer be a seeker, but simply live in the consciousness of God. He is always present in every moment. All you have to do is stop and feel.

83

*Strength and kindness
living side by side.*

Grace

To live gracefully is to be in harmony and integrity with yourself and your world. It is a culmination of many things coming into proper alignment, bringing polarity to sweet balance.

The Grace of God is a force we can open to, that will draw the beauty and lightness in us. When we feel connected to the Divine, guided by his will, held by his force, we are able to blossom and offer our own sweet fragrance.

Grace can be seen and felt in the elegance of the natural world; the sweet dance of the celestial bodies, the blossoms of our flowers, and the majesty of birds in flight.

Embody grace, be in grace, move with grace. Strength and kindness living side by side.

84

*Embody the teachings
for them to become real.*

Make it Real

Our religions and spiritual teachings speak of resting in the love and power of God. For many, this sounds wonderful, but not really possible.

It is through our devotional and spiritual practices that we cultivate a personal connection to the Divine within. Sitting in stillness and going beyond the fears and limitations of our ego mind takes us into a whole new reality, which allows us to rest knowing that we are held and guided by a higher force than our limited self.

We need to embody the teachings for them to become real. A personal transformation is what we are looking for. There is quite a difference between reading a travel book about an exotic place or even watching a movie filmed there and the actual experience of being there. It requires a complete immersion to fully experience our potential.

It is a simple shift in awareness that allows us to see and feel the Divine all around us, which in turn changes everything in our lives. Dedication and a burning desire to break through the illusion of lack and separation is what is required.

Real transformation tends to take place through the "dark nights of the soul", when we reach a place of total surrender and we truly feel the need to become open to the higher power. We must stop the personal control and struggle to feel the gentle wind of the Divine.

We can choose to open through the pressure cooker of life's challenges until we collapse and surrender, or we can cultivate that in us with the gentle steam of a focused and consistent practice.

85

*Your light
will speak for you.*

Illumination

Become a crystal vase and allow the Divine light within to be expressed through your uniqueness.

Let the murky water settle into the bottom and sit in the clear stillness of your being.

Open to God and place the future in his hands. Be the child in awe with the world embracing the mystery that accompanies each moment.

Observe your emotions and let them be calmed by your love. Savor the stillness that lives within you.

Your light will speak for you. It will drive every thought and action. You will live as a transparent reflection of the Divine. Love and joy will live as you!

86

There is a place within us that is full of love and peace, where we experience the wholeness of our being and the interconnectedness of all that exists.

The Oasis is Real

We have it backwards. Life is the illusion and the oasis is what is actually real.

There is a place within us that is full of love and peace, where we experience the wholeness of our being and the interconnectedness of all that exists.

Our minds give us the illusion of lack and fear. It blinds us from the paradise that dwells inside of us.

We must calm our minds and open our hearts with our spiritual practices. Heaven and hell exist side by side. By our thoughts and actions, we create the world that we personally inhabit.

A calm person is able to chose love over fear. A stilled mind can see into the horizon. An open heart can understand the suffering of others and stay centered in itself.

Our practices can create a super highway to our oasis. We start bushwhacking our way there, and with steady practice, it simply becomes a way of being.

87

*Open your heart to the magic
of something greater than yourself.*

You Are Not Alone

There is a place that you can go, where you are loved and accepted as you fully are. Your fears and your pain are understood and dissolved as you enter the realm of the Divine.

You are not alone. You are not at the mercy of a cruel world, but you can get lost in the stories and fears of your mind.

Open your heart to the magic of something greater than yourself. All the mystics have pointed to this oasis where you can rest and rejoice. This place exists within you and it can be reached through an open heart held in the present moment.

Your mind tricks you into feeling lack and alone, while the whole universe is here holding and supporting you in every moment of your life. No matter how dark the clouds become or how large the storm may seem, if you stay focused and connected to the light beyond the storm, you will get to the other side with a peace that dwells beyond your simple understanding.

Within every problem the solution already exists. There is a process and a journey that you are here to experience and Divine timing is always at play. Feel and trust the guidance you are receiving all along the way. Stop and replenish in the oasis within yourself.

88

There is the seen and the unseen world.

Between Worlds

As humans we inhabit multiple realities simultaneously. There is the seen and the unseen worlds. Our thoughts and emotions create one reality. And there is the physcical world before us. We live in a small spectrum of energy perceived by our senses and we have access to the whole of the Universe by our consciousness.

Science has let us see and understand forces that our naked eyes can not see. Our modern medicine is based on microorganisms and cell structures only detected by intricate technology. Understanding the invisible law of gravity has enabled us to conquer space.

Also hidden from our vision is the energy that holds all of us in unity. The mystics and sages based their knowledge and teachings on their knowledge of this very real force. This energy goes by many names; Holy Spirit, Grace, Shakti, the Great Spirit. Creating a direct connection to this force is our highest calling.

There is no need for a "leap of faith". Our job is to lean into this force and learn to navigate our lives with its wisdom. We can become intimate with the force behind all of existence by gently listening and following its subtle flow. We can actively align and surrender to the wisdom of the moment. Fear and control separates us from source.

There is no place that this force is not present, for it is all. Yet, we can choose to never see it. We can live solely in the realm of our ego-self looking for all our answers in the manifested world or we can choose to see the energy from which the whole world is created and sustained. Here lies God consciousness in all its beauty and glory.

Training our minds through meditation opens a window into this inner world. By pulling our senses inward we can expand our reality as we open a direct experience of the consciousness that lies behind our thinking mind.

All the tools we need are already in us. Knowing where to look and developing the mental muscles will take us to a whole new world from which to live our lives. Harmony, integrity, love, joy, health, and abundance all dwell within us. Our job is to align to our highest vibration.

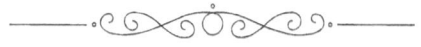

89

*Trust your instincts
and
follow your desires.*

Our Creative Power

We are here to express ourselves, to expand into new experiences and ways of interacting with our world. There is a force within us that is restless and always looking for something new, wanting to explore the different flavors available to us.

Life is always looking for the sun. There is a force inside all living beings that is looking to survive, to expand, and to thrive. Align to this innate force and make life an adventure vacation.

Do you know how hard it is to keep weeds out of the garden? To hold back nature in any sustainable way? It is the same with us. The only thing keeping us small is our own selves. Our doubts and fears block our light and diminish the life force that wants to express itself.

Trust your instincts and follow your desires. Not necessarily for material things but for who you would like to be. What will make you happy? Don't look for recognition, fame, or outer success. Take the time to discover and nourish what brings joy to your heart.

The universe is always expanding. It is God's immense garden finding harmony and expression in all of creation. Take your place as an individual ray of light, reaching to freely share your beauty and magnificence with all that cross your path.

Respect everyone's opinion, including your own, and follow the gentle whisper of your heart into the highest expression of your unique self.

90

*We create heaven or hell on earth
by the thoughts we think and the actions we take.*

Master Creators

We are master creators. In every moment we bring to life our own version of reality. We are powerful beings, bringing our thoughts and ideas into manifestation. We are alchemists able to transform ourselves and our lives at the speed of our thoughts.

Take a moment to acknowledge the power that has been given to us over our lives. We reign over our reality, we can choose to see good or evil, love or hate, lack or abundance, and in so choosing, we create what we experience and share with the world.

Making the choice to align and be in harmony with our world brings peace and stillness to our reality. Exploring our inner universe gives us direct connection to the Divine that lives within.

We are not victims, unless we make that our choice. We are free to choose our path and every choice has its challenges and rewards. We reap what we sow and we always have the choice to change what we bring into our garden.

Wake up and become the master of your destiny. Do the work to connect and honor your heart's desires. Align with Grace and follow your bliss. Become the bright light that is your birth right.

Don't be afraid of your magnificence. Lean into your potential and let Grace create the path before your feet. Flex your muscles of creation and receive the blessings that are waiting for you.

Make the choice to be happy, to love and support those around you. Share your bounty and rejoice in the blessings of others. We create heaven or hell on earth by the thoughts we think and the actions we take.

91

*To find your true self you need to let go
and move beyond all the things you identify with.
You need to lose yourself to actually find
your true essence.*

Find Yourself

Who are you really? There are many things that belong to you, but you are much more than your parts. You go by a certain name, you have roles you play with others in life; son, mother, spouse, boss, employee, friend...
You have a body with certain characteristics and you belong to some ethnic group, but who are you really?

You are pure light, pure potential, expressing itself in time and space. Your emotions are all related to the ego identity from which you are living. Connect to the light within that is your only constant. Peace, love and joy are your true essence.

To find your true self you need to let go and move beyond all the things you identify with. You need to lose yourself to actually find your true essence.

We are born naked and full of potential. We can become anything and everything our hearts' desire. Slowly we start adding onto ourselves, beliefs that start defining who we are. With everything we choose to take on, there are endless other possibilities that we have now left out.

Soon we have tightly defined ourselves with many characteristics that limit and hide all that we truly are. We see ourselves and our world from this box we have created. We become but a fraction of our true potential.

We can loosen the chains of our ego identification by deliberate practice of meditation and contemplation. We can once again become identified with that blank slate from where we started. Anything we have put on, we can take off.

In stillness you can hear the gentle whisper to come home, to return to your true self.

92

*Trust the unseen,
the unheard,
and enjoy the ride!*

Enjoy the Mystery

Feel the magic and the mystery that is inherent in every moment. The unknown surrounds us and unfolds into reality one moment at a time. Nothing is certain. We may have expectations for a probable future, but there are no guarantees in life.

We have learned to trust the unfolding of the days and nights and the changing of the seasons. We surrender to the cycles of nature, swaying with its ebb and flow.

In our lives, we are accustomed to releasing control to those we trust. My students get into complicated and challenging poses following my instructions. They surrender to the class experience. We surrender and place our lives in the hands of the airplane pilot and the surgeon, and we relax knowing we are not in charge.

Can you take this to the next level and surrender your fears and control to the magic within the mystery? Can you soften and relax in this moment knowing that all is in Divine order?

You are here now because the mystery has never let you down. The next moment arrived giving you what you needed to experience to help you grow and evolve into the person you have become, the person you are becoming.

If we place all of our attention on what is occurring in each moment, we are able to fully experience the beauty and the gifts which make up our lives. It is our need to control and manipulate that takes us away from our natural state of contentment and appreciation. Trust the unseen, the unheard, and enjoy the ride!

93

*Create positive wealth
in all aspects of your life.*

Our Bank Account

Let's think of the Universe as this huge bank where we make deposits and withdrawals. What actually gets deposited are our thoughts and actions and all we can retrieve is what we have put into it.

If our thoughts are negative and our feelings are those of lack and struggle, that is all that is available for us to use in the future. We have to be mindful of what we are creating and what we are emphasizing in our lives, because this will continue to compound and be the currency we have to use in creating our future.

We have to create in us that which we want to experience and have in our lives. It takes effort to change our habitual patterns of thinking and acting, but once we start to become aware of our habits and we begin making small changes, the whole process becomes easier.

As we start creating more currency of love and peace, as we bring more gratitude and abundance into our thinking and actions, they become the energy from which we relate to life and which life returns to us, with interest.

It simply makes no sense to cultivate and maintain feelings and emotions that are not life affirming. Look for the light and the beauty around you. Make the choices that come from love and generosity. Create positive wealth in all aspects of your life.

The best part of this universal bank is that we can instantly draw out what we just deposited. A lifetime of negative thoughts and actions can be corrected by our internal shift. Love immediately generates more love. At any moment our whole lives can change once we choose to make that change.

Nothing is beyond our reach because it all exists inside of us. It is a matter of bringing it out.

94

*Be love,
see the love,
share the love.*

There is nothing but love!

Loving Love

Love truly makes the world go round. Our lives are colored in the most magnificent of ways if we deepen into its many shades.

Love sits behind our fears and our need to control. It is a constant energy that nurtures and appreciates the beauty that surrounds us. It asks for nothing and sees the beautiful side of any situation.

When we are full, contented, in any moment, it is because love has been allowed to rise to the top. It stops all cravings and nurtures us at our deepest level.

Fall in love with the energy of love. Take it with you wherever you go. Share it freely as it is never ending.

Shades of love are found in all emotions; they are the base energy of all creation. See the love found in pain, in sadness, in grief, and in anger. Once you see it, it will transmute the situation into its most beautiful expression.

Be naked and vulnerable as it will expand your capacity for love. Share your dreams and fears and see them transformed. See others as they are and let them see your own complexity and contradictions. Love does not need to judge and separate. Love simply sees the beauty and comforts our human insecurities.

Seek the love within yourself. Let it dance and move through you. Become an instrument of its transformational power as it is shared with others.

Be love, see the love, share the love. There is nothing but love!

95

*Slow down,
feel the hand of God
guiding you in every moment.*

Living Without Fear

Can you imagine a world where your actions are not guided by a sensation of lack or a fear of an uncertain future? A place with no grasping, no controlling, no tension, no fear?

Imagine living in a world controlled by doting parents who pampered, protected, and indulged you in all the things that would support your life journey. Are you willing to open up to the awareness that this life is such a place?

Slow down, feel the hand of God guiding you in every moment. Feel his breath breathing you. Know the current that sustains you.

Don't behave like drowning children in a shallow pool. Stand in the power of the Divine. It is as solid as the Earth we walk on. It is as dependable as the Sun and the Moon.

Fear is our biggest motivator. It makes us do many things that we would rather not do. We do them from a place of need and lack. Imagine living your whole life from a place of generosity, gifting your time and energy, sharing your love and efforts because you want to.

Our thoughts and feelings are the language in which we communicate with the creator. It can only give us what we choose to accept. All the joy, peace, abundance and health is available to us. It is our inheritance and our Divine nature.

As you can take a horse to water but can't make him drink, it is the same with us. We have free will to live our lives as we choose. We can walk away and turn our backs on our highest potential, or we can actively choose to align to the Grace that nurtures and supports us. Relax and release into its power and rejoice in the glory of God.

96

*You can walk through life like a King that is
free from outer entanglements,
laughing and dancing in the abundance that
lives in your heart, secure in the true strength that
only comes from within.*

Inner Strength vs Outer Power

As part of my life journey, I have experienced substantial wealth and complete financial loss on more than one occasion. I've had the experience of having to leave behind the country into which I was born, Cuba. I have had two home fires where I lost all of my personal possessions and two divorces from which I have started new lives.

Through our spiritual practices we can cultivate a sense of Self that is separate from our possessions and our ego attachments. We cultivate an inner knowing and strength that does not rely on the outer circumstances of our lives.

Our strength comes from our relationship with the Divine energy that lives within us and that supports us always throughout our lives. If we place our trust on the external wealth we have created, there is always a sense of fear and lack. Is there enough? If the market changes will we be ok?

Developing that direct connection to the abundance of the Universe gives us a sense of deep peace, because it is not dependent on outer circumstances. We ride the ebb and flow of change knowing that our path is Divinely guided and that we will always have more than enough.

There is no need to hoard or be greedy if we can sit in the knowing that we will be provided for. Neither your identity nor self worth is tied up in fledgling worldly success.

You can walk through life like a King that is free from outer entanglements, laughing and dancing in the abundance that lives in your heart, secure in the true strength that only comes from within.

97

*We are all one and we are all unique,
perfect in our imperfections.*

One Absolute Truth

There is one absolute truth and the rest is subjective reality.

It is human nature to get caught-up in the small things of life. We can argue about a tree and not understand its place in the harmony of the whole forest. If a truth is absolute, all perspectives must hold true even when they are in opposition to one another.

Our understanding must be broad enough to include all the potential experiences. The sages and masters have all held this expansive knowing and now our current science is explaining it in ways that our mind can begin to comprehend.

We live in a world understood by comparison. We know things in relationship to its opposite; black and white, hot and cold. Yet opposites are just levels of the same energy. Polarity lives within unity.

The path of the mystic and the yogi is to go beyond intellectual understanding into direct experience. It is embodying the light and the truth.

Through our devotional practices and dedication to our spiritual paths, we cultivate levels of silence and stillness that allow us to perceive what is normally hidden behind the noise of our minds. We travel beyond the identity of our ego to experience the pulse that sustains the Universe. We feel the energy web, the canvas, that holds all manifested forms - the black sky holds all the planets and suns, all the celestial bodies.

We are all one and we are all unique, perfect in our imperfections. We can use movement to find the still point and in silence we enter our expansive inner universe. Religions divide us and yet they all point to our center. Actually, all paths ultimately lead to our centers, some are more direct than others.

Prayer, meditation, and contemplation will all light your path home. Discover the absolute truth that lives within you!

98

*The outer world is but a reflection of our inner being.
The inside creates the outside,
they are one and the same.*

Create From Within

Our lives are about expressing and becoming. We have God's desire to create and to experience as our driving force. Our fears and limiting beliefs will distort and diminish our potential, so a great part of our work is to purify our beings of these subconscious patterns.

Looking to the outer world and measuring ourselves by material accomplishments is less effective than paying attention to our inner states of being. Follow activities that bring joy to you, be with people that are positive and up-lifting, eat healthy and stay active.

Cultivate who you are, not what you have. What are the qualities that you value in others? Draw them out in yourself.

You are the canvas and the masterpiece that is to be created over a lifetime. Start transforming fear into love, and selfishness into generosity, let kindness and compassion be your default state.

As we change from the inside, it will directly affect how we interact with the world. The outer world is but a reflection of our inner being. The inside creates the outside, they are one and the same.

Refining yourself allows your highest gifts to come to the surface. With love and contentment in your being you will be able to freely offer and express your deep reservoir of light and creative energy to the world. It is the only way to fulfill your dharma (life purpose) to its greatest potential.

Decide each morning to be the best version of yourself. No need to be judgmental, simply start moving in the right direction. Small steps every day will transform anything and everything.

99

*The path of least resistance is the one in which you
follow your hearts' desires,
in harmony and service to the world.*

The Path of Least Resistance

Have you ever wondered why there is so much effort and struggle in the world, in your life? Sometimes it feels like everyone is purposely going against the current, willfully trying to impose their desires and will on the world around them, or simply trying to survive as if sinking in quick sand.

Imagine a world where you did not compete or impose your will on others, where everyone is respected and we all feel safe being ourselves.

This world begins within each of us. We must accept and invite the individuality in all of us to come to expression. This will allow us to experience the magnitude of that, which actually unites us.

You are in the flow of life if you are following your passion. Your efforts will not feel like work. They will simply be an expression of your love and your being. Your body may be tired, but you will not feel drained or exhausted. You will work hard but you will have restful sleep.

The path of least resistance is the one in which you follow your hearts' desires. It is not you against the world, but you in harmony and service to the world. Cultivate trust in the wisdom of each moment and let your actions come from love and acceptance.

Move like the wind, gently touching all in your path. See the harmony that surrounds you. Choose kindness and sincerity and your life will begin to move with the effortless flow of Grace.

It is your choice to be in opposition or in harmony. Don't allow fear to dictate your choices. Trust in the Divine and be the light of your own being.

100

*Slow down and listen,
feel and savor
what is here and now.*

Feel Each Moment

Every second is filled with wisdom and information. All we need to know and all we need to be, is contained in each moment of time. Slow down and listen, feel and savor what is here and now.

It takes practice and determination not to be swept away by the constant flow of thoughts and emotions. The mind is always ready to take us away on a journey toward an unknown future or a rehash of the past.

Our capacity for love and joy, for creativity and fulfillment, is directly related to our ability to feel and connect with each moment. Learn to savor without distortion all the bounty that is in your life right now.

There is a sweetness to each breath we take and a bond of love with those traveling with us. A celebration occurs each day with the rising of the sun. A stillness and restfulness glides in as the days come to an end.

Sing with the morning birds, and enjoy the blessings that each day brings! Open to the Grace that sustains each day and enjoy this gift called life.

Turn each day into an offering of love and service. There is an inner knowing that honors the highest expression in each moment. Don't allow guilt, fear, or lack to guide your day. Go deeper and beyond those surface emotions to the love and light that lives within you, in the silence and stillness of your being.

Soften, soften, soften… sink into your Self and savor this moment!

101

*The bliss
is in the dance.*

Make Love with Life

The Divine comes alive through all of existence. Love and light express themselves through all living things. The Garden of Eden is still intact and lives within each of us.

By harmonizing polarity, uniting opposites within ourselves and others, we come to experience reality as it truly is.

Practice making love with life, have direct connection with reality. Feel, touch, and savor the here and now. Harmonize your life to the rhythm of your breath and you will bind in Divine intimacy. A good lover does not impose his or her own will, he or she simply rides the waves of shared awareness and pleasure. The bliss is in the dance.

It is through our practices that we realize the potential of the scriptures. It is an active surrender to the flow of life. The dance and the dancer become one, nothing else exists. Here lies the promised land.

Create equanimity by resting in the moment. There is no need to search nor strive; just rest in reality, in the harmony of your breath, in the rhythm of your heart.

102

*Being a yogi
is becoming fully engaged and balanced
within all the ebbs and flows that life offers.*

Yoga is not Exercise

You can exercise in a yogic way, but exercise is not yoga, even if you are doing typical yoga poses. Yoga is about cultivating and creating a union within polarity, bringing all parts of ourselves to a moment of time and having a profound intimate experience with what is occurring in each moment.

Being a yogi is becoming fully engaged and balanced within all the ebbs and flows that life offers. It is a joyful ride on the rollercoaster of life.

All of the tools we use in yoga are only to help us experience what is already within us. There is no effort or striving needed to experience the yogic state. We prepare ourselves to receive the Grace that engulfs us.

If you are getting hurt by your physical yoga practice you are over effort-ing. You are willfully pushing beyond your healthy balance.

We all want to remain active and have healthy, strong bodies. We want to have sharp, clear minds with healthy emotions. These qualities can be attained separate or in conjunction with our yogic practices.

Know the difference as they are profoundly divergent ways from which to experience life. One is willful and ego centered and the other is in harmony and in service to the Divine within and without.

103

*We surrender our small will
to be in harmony and service to
the Divine will.*

Nirvana

It is important not to confuse the practices and tools of the yogic path for the state of being that we want to embody.

All the tools are meant to help us navigate to a place where we can open to the highest level of ourselves that already lives within us.

The highest gifts of yoga arrive by Grace. We can not make them happen, we simply practice becoming more intimate with ourselves and with life.

Ha-tha yoga helps us to integrate the polarity of our being. Meditation practices help us to cultivate the witness consciousness in us. They are great tools for understanding ourselves and bringing balance to our lives.

Beyond these practices is opening to a state of union with the life force that creates and sustains all. There is an active surrender to the beauty and joy of the here and now. We surrender our small will to be in harmony and service to the Divine will.

God's promise of the Garden of Eden is available to us in this lifetime. Cultivate your inner garden by putting your spiritual path first. Follow the well-lit path toward a place of personal connection and intimacy with yourself and your life.

Feel the Divine in you and around you. Trust the life journey that you have been given. Fully and actively surrender your ego agenda to engage in the fullness of each moment.

There is no joy in controlling or being fearful. We must become children, completely trusting the love and safety provided by our parent, the creator of the Universe, our God.

104

*Let the breath have its way with you.
You will discover a freedom and a lightness of being
beyond your imagination.*

The Mystical Breath

Be with your breath and you are with God. In yoga asana practice the breath is what creates the pose. Follow the breath as it expresses itself through you.

Learn to connect and follow the breath as it creates each expression of life. Cultivate intimacy by slowing down and aligning to the energy that creates and sustains all. Be one with the ebb and flow of life.

Through the breath, you have direct experience of the stillness within motion, of creation and dissolution, of allowing. Let the breath have its way with you. You will discover a freedom and a lightness of being beyond your imagination.

Something is living you, looking out for you, healing you. It is an extreme intelligence, a mystery. This complete love no one can give nor take away from you. It lives within you as you.

105

*The source of the Universe is expressed
through all things.
Lets celebrate our uniqueness within the divinity
that unites us.*

God is All - All is God

The source of the Universe is expressed through all things. It puts on a disguise to express all sorts of expressions of itself, but don't be fooled as it all comes from the same fundamental energy.

The Divine simply puts on different outer garments, whether it becomes a star, a planet, a fish, or one of us, it is still the creator playing in his kingdom.

Train your mind to see God in all things, in all situations, and you will peak into the Truth of reality.

We are not alone. There is no lack. Love is the foundation that sustains all of existence. We just need to see it. By opening our hearts, our inner eyes can see the unity of life.

Lets celebrate our uniqueness within the Divinity that unites us.

106

*Heaven is right here, right now.
Nothing needs to be created,
it is waiting to be revealed.*

Stop Seeking - Start Seeing

We are programmed to feel that we are incomplete. Something is always missing and it is to be found in the future. We are to seek God, pray for health and abundance, become a better version of ourselves, create a better life…. all of that, in an uncertain future.

The truth is that it is only in this moment that we can actually find and experience that which we are desiring. Don't look for God in your spiritual teachings, but see it right now in the world that surrounds us; in the miracle of life, in the eyes and the smile of another.

Only by deepening our experience of this moment can we grasp what is fully occurring right now. By always keeping our eyes in the future, we miss what is already here.

When we change our perspective, we change our vision and a new reality becomes available. Don't look for God, see God now. Don't ask for blessings, just receive them in the same way we take our breath, drink our water, and eat our food.

Savor each moment as if you were seated in the best restaurant in the world and the chef was bringing his delicacies for you to experience. All your senses would be alive, you would chew slowly and explore the textures and subtle tastes. You would make the evening last and be delighted by the experience.

Heaven is right here, right now. It is hidden behind your fears, your need to control, and your sense of separation. Simply stop grasping and start savoring the experiences in your life now and a new reality will unfold right before your eyes. Nothing needs to be created, it is waiting to be revealed.

107

*Having a personal and direct connection to
this inner light transforms your existence.
Fear and the sense of separation are replaced by a deep
love and appreciation for the life you have been gifted.*

Inner Light

There is a light within us that is always radiant. This light comforts us with a deep sense of peace and stillness. It is the light from the mind of God that we share as our birthright. It has always been and will always be there as our beacon home.

When we fill our minds up with grievances, stress, and ego desires we literally create clouds in front of this inner sun. We block the nourishing energy that is there to sustain us.

As spiritual beings, our first priority is to be connected to and in the flow of this Divine energy. Within it lies true love and peace from which to experience a healthy life of contentment and abundance.

If we place our petty concerns between us and this inner light, we are truly living in darkness and ignorance. We are chasing shadows to fill that emptiness that lies within us.

By maintaining a daily practice of meditation and contemplation we develop mastery over our minds. We can hold back the thoughts that tie us to our grievances and we can open to the mystery that lives within our consciousness.

All it takes is dedication and persistence to learn to journey to the source that lives within you. Having a personal and direct connection to this inner light transforms your existence. Fear and the sense of separation are replaced by a deep love and appreciation for the life you have been gifted.

108

Connect to the Divine current.
Allow its energy and light to flow through us.
Sustained from within, we can let go of our fears
and align our lives to our highest good.

Just Plug In

There is really just one solution to our human conditioning and that is to simply plug into the Divine current. This one action brings everything into alignment.

We tend to see ourselves as separate and independent. From this vantage point, its a scary world out there and we feel a need to take control and protect ourselves and our loved ones. We don't see ourselves as part of a system in which we are all sustained by the creator of the Universes.

Our job is to connect to the Divine current and allow its energy and light to flow through us. Sustained from within, we can let go of our fears and align our lives to our highest good. All that exists in our world exists in harmony with the life force.

A seed once planted simply begins to grow into its potential, it does not question whether or not to follow the sun. Birds migrate in alignment with the seasons, they don't question the rhythm of the planet. We humans are the only beings that can decide whether to align, to plug in to the Divine current or continue to identify ourselves as separate from the energy that created us and sustains us. We are like waves that have forgotten that we are connected to, and a part of the majestic ocean.

This current is pure love, it is the force that birthed the Universes. It has the unconditional love of a mother that simply wants us to be happy, to experience our wildest dreams, to savor and enjoy our gift of being alive.

Without plugging in we are like a lamp with no electricity, maybe running on a dim battery powered by our own lack, fears and desires. Once we tap into the Universal current we can light up the world, we are complete within ourselves, so we can fully share and love.

We are either tapped into the energy of love or we are in fear. If we feel separate, then we are not complete, we feel needy, lacking in some way. This feeling of separation is the ailment of our human conditioning. It is the root cause of all the actions that are endangering our world.

Through a daily devotional spiritual practice we can breakaway from this false sense of separation and come to the direct realization of our oneness.

As we all plug back into the love energy that creates and sustains all there is, we are released from the ignorance of perceiving ourselves separate. Our fears, anxieties, tension, dis-ease, will simply melt away as we let our lives be sustained and guided by this inner current. We can then move with love and passion to express our highest potential.

We can spend our whole lives, if not many lifetimes, searching outside of ourselves for happiness and fulfillment. We can amass fortunes, go through a multitude of lovers, experience everything and anything in excess and still there will be an emptiness in our being. The only action that will satisfy this emptiness is to fully plug into the love current of the Universe.

The best part is that its already in us. It is already sustaining us. All we need to do is recognize it and allow it to shine brighter by not blocking it.

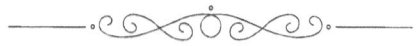

109

*Experience the world from the eyes of your heart,
taste the flavors of your experiences,
but never forget you are light.*

I am Light... Experiencing Life

Light puts on thoughts, emotions, a physical body and goes into the world. It never stops being light, it just dresses up for the occasion.

Every day, take the time to undress and touch the essence of your being. Choose the thoughts and emotions that will serve you the best. See the world as it really is.

Experience the world from the eyes of your heart, taste the flavors of your experiences, but never forget you are light.

In the stillness of meditation we can shed the thoughts that make us feel weak and alone, and we can experience our radiant sun.

In the tears and the joy of our brothers and sisters, we can see the spark of the Divine.

Our light hides in plain sight.

110

*Refining and silencing our ego
to the point that we can transcend it,
leads us to a direct experience of the Divine in us.*

This is the yogic path of knowledge and liberation.

One Problem One Solution

We spend our lives going from one challenge to the next always trying to find a solution for what ails us. It can be relationships, finances, careers, health issues, depression or a simple lack of direction in our lives. There is the false feeling that once we take care of "this" all will be well. But that day never arrives.

Only by identifying the root cause of our ailments can we change our condition. The Yogis call it "ignorance" which seemed like a very harsh word when I first encountered it in this context. With further study the full meaning made much sense to me. They describe it as our human state of not knowing our own divinity. It is the human state described in Christian language as Original Sin. It is the point when we begin to see ourselves separate from God and God's will as it expresses itself through us.

Modern psychology and new age spirituality make a lot of arguments that self love is the key to a healthier and happier life, but I feel it still falls quite short of our true potential.

True love and peace can only be achieved by cultivating the direct experience of our innate connection to the Universal force that we call God. Our ego desires and fears create a veil that blocks our direct knowledge of the light the dwells in us.

Refining and silencing our ego to the point that we can transcend it, leads us to a direct experience of the Divine in us. This is the yogic path of knowledge and liberation. It is the solution to our fundamental problem of perceived separation from our source.

111

Know that you don't know.
Move into the mystery with no preconceptions.

BE STILL... LISTEN

Be still, drop into yourself and listen to the whisper within. The ego's voice is loud and restless, and yet beyond it, is the deepest love and peace you could imagine.

There are many tools, techniques to help quiet your thoughts but your intention will determine what fruits you receive from your efforts. Ask for nothing less than connecting to the mind of God that lives within you and in which you exist.

Going beyond your thoughts opens the veil to existence. Truth frees us from your fears and limitations. Learn to listen without projecting your beliefs, your religion, our desires. Go beyond your beliefs by asking for our true nature to be revealed. Know that you don't know.

Be still, listen with an open mind, move into the mystery with no preconceptions. Immerse yourself in the light that dwells within. Only then can the Divine be revealed to you.

112

*Bring your head below your heart,
surrender your intellect, to the wisdom of the heart.*

Bow

Bow to the Divine force within, to the creator of all there is, to the source energy of pure love.

Bring your head below your heart, surrender your intellect, to the wisdom of the heart.

Know that you don't know, and open to something beyond your comprehension.

Humble and naked of thoughts and desires, receive the truth that lies within.

Let stillness fill your being and be one with all there is… Love!

113

Develop the habit and strength of remaining solid and connected to your deepest self no matter what is occurring in the outer world.

Draw into Your Center

Our yoga practice teaches us that in order to remain grounded and stable in our poses we need to use our muscles in a way that stabilizes our skeletal system and hugs the center of our bodies. We can take this awareness off the mat and incorporate it into our lives.

Life's challenges have a way of pulling us out of our stable inner self. By creating a daily practice of flexing our mental and emotional muscles, we can develop the habit and strength of remaining solid and connected to our deepest selves no matter what is occurring in the outer world.

By exploring our physical bodies with poses that require balance, strength and flexibility, we develop an awareness of how to be both grounded and stable while remaining soft and receptive.

Our meditation and breath-work draws us into a deep awareness of our fundamental nature. When we take the noise out of ourselves, we are left with the pure essence of being.

Feeling these qualities in ourselves, we can recognize the loss of that state, when confronted with people or situations that destabilize us.

Our whole lives are a journey of self knowledge and exploration. Many times our focus is just on the outer accomplishments or goals, while in reality it is the inner evolution that really matters and what ultimately creates the outer change.

Take the time to cultivate the skills that lead to states of wellbeing. A healthy body and a calm mind are the foundations for a fulfilling and joyful life.

114

*Learn to explore and follow
your own version of the path.
Each one of your steps is uniquely yours.*

Footprints

Walking alone on the beach I could see footprints of those that had come before me. They showed the well traveled path along the seashore.

I was reminded how we have many spiritual teachers that have left their footprints by way of the teachings and scriptures we study and follow. They got there before us and chose to mark the path to make the journey easier and more direct for us.

Being grateful for our teachers, we also must learn to explore and follow our own version of the path. Their teachings can serve as a north star but each one of our steps is uniquely ours.

Strictly following a teachers' footprints only leads us to their door. It becomes a dead path. A great teacher points the way for our personal evolutions assisting us in finding our own unique expression of what is possible.

115

*Only in silence
can we truly hear and experience
our Divine nature.*

Yoga: Shift in Consciousness

The path of Yoga is aimed at training our minds to experience a totally new reality. One that is not driven by lack, fear, and a sense of separation, but instead, has a direct experience of the oneness of existence.

Through meditation and contemplation we can go beyond our ego centered experiences of this world. We can clearly see how our beliefs limit what is possible in each moment, how we block the Divine potential in us. Pure joy is being kept at bay.

God's consciousness is real and we have direct access to it. It is our birthright to live in its grace and glory.

We have enslaved ourselves by giving our ego-mind dominion over our lives. The truth has been hidden behind our endless array of thoughts. God speaks in the silence of our minds.

Our energy and effort is mostly directed to managing our outer world, while the key to life is in becoming masters of ourselves. Love, harmony, peace, stillness, contentment, health, joy, and abundance are all states of mind. They can not be found in possessions or external circumstances.

Releasing our need to control the outer circumstances lets us move into the inner peace found beyond our ego-selves. We block God's grace when we choose to struggle and control. We must learn to soften into the mystery of each moment. Only in silence can we truly hear and experience our Divine nature.

116

*We are the instruments that play the Divine music of
creation and dissolution,
and the notes that we play are dependent on the quality
of our thought patterns.*

Formless Form

We are all part of this cosmic dance of light and love moving from pure potential to manifested form, forming and dissolving through time and space. We are filters of this light, creating unique expressions of Divine manifestation. All is possible, and there is no distinction from our ideas of "good or bad". Everything just is.

Our true nature is this creative force and we are simply dancing in our impermanent manifestations. We are the instruments that play the Divine music of creation and dissolution, and the notes that we play are dependent on the quality of our thought patterns.

All of our interpretations, actions, and manifestations travel through our states of mind and our subconscious beliefs. The quality of who we are, and what we express is driven by these invisible forces deep in our consciousness.

Beliefs and patterns of experience acquired in our early childhoods will run our shows for the rest of our lives, unless we take steps to free ourselves. Our innate freedom is restricted by our limiting beliefs.

Bringing small shifts into our perspective, opens the door to new expressions and possibilities for ourselves.

Just remembering that we are co-creators of our lives, and that in every moment we have the opportunity to grow and see things differently, opens us to states of joyful expression and expansion.

117

*No dream is too high and no step is too small
in leading us towards the birth of our creations.
We must dream and we must act
to bear fruits in our lives.*

Dream

Our minds are pregnant with endless possibilities. We can close our eyes and explore any situation or reality we care to bring into ourselves. Infinite virtual reality exists within each of us.

As co-creators we literally bring down our ideas and if they are powerful enough we manifest them in our lives. It is what we consciously or unconsciously do every moment of our existence.

Our culture is not very supportive of "day dreamers" and we are told to forget our fantasies and to get real, be practical, conform, and live a sheep's life. Yet, we are meant to express our deepest desires, our gifts from the Divine.

Our conscious mind can only create what it knows from past experiences. To be fully creative and alive we must reach beyond our current knowledge and draw from the wisdom that lies inside of us.

We must dare to dream and create beauty and joy, to express and enjoy heaven on Earth. The dreamers and thinkers propel our shared consciousness into higher levels of living. It is our birthright and responsibility to add to this quilt of creation.

No dream is too high and no step is too small in leading us towards the birth of our creations. But we must dream and we must act to bear fruits in our lives.

We lived in this magical place as children, our imaginations ran wild and we played with abandonment just for the joy of it all… That magic still lives within and it's asking us to "come out and play!"

118

*We are both the light and the shadow
weaving our impermanent creations.
Dancing through time and space
between the real and the unreal.*

Light Dancing in the World of Shadows

We spend our lives chasing shadows looking for truth. In this world of impermanence we look to leave a legacy, looking for some sort of immortality. We are obsessed with building castles in the sand.

Recognize that we are the light that creates the shadows, and become free of the insanity that is our world. So many search for answers inside of the question, unable to stand back and see the whole picture.

Our religions, our stories, our identifications hold us entrenched in the shadows. We are our own jailers trapped in our self created illusions.

You hold the key to Divine freedom. All it takes is the willingness to leave the shadows behind. Let your inner light burn through the veil of the unreal and know that you are embodied light.

Paradoxically, the journey toward the light is accomplished by going inwards, into the depths of our being. By emptying ourselves of the outer entrapments we find the light that frees us.

We are both the light and the shadow weaving our impermanent creations. Dancing through time and space between the real and the unreal. Playing hide and seek in the game we call life.

119

*Stay light.
Keep it simple.*

Traveling Through Life

Our lives are a journey through space and time. We are in constant motion as a new year, a new season, a new day, a new moment is constantly coming into existence. Each day is unfolding for us to engage and explore.

We enter the world alone and we will leave the world alone. In between those two places there will be lots of new people and things that will come into our lives and that will also leave. Change is the only constant in our existence on earth.

If we learn to flow with the natural cycle of creation, sustaining, dissolution, the pause (that is empty/full), and then a new creation, we will have much more inner peace and greater joy.

Can we treat life like an extended journey? If we are traveling we tend to choose places we would like to visit. We stay a while if it feels good, then we move on to the next location. When traveling, I am pulled to explore and appreciate the time that I am in a location, aware that I will be moving on, that it will end. I enjoy meeting new people, but I don't get attached and try to take them along. If we are traveling in the same direction, we can travel together, but I don't cling to them beyond our allotted travel time.

As an experienced traveler you also learn that you don't need very much. Actually, you learn that it is a real burden to carry any more than what you truly need. Staying light, keeping it simple, allows for greater freedom.

Take a look at your life and identify all the things and people that you are holding onto beyond their time. All of that is slowing you down, stopping you from moving forward on your life's journey. If they are meant to be traveling with you now, it will feel life-affirming and supportive. If it is dead weight, unburden yourself!

120

*We dive into the bliss of the unknown
to discover all that is truly real.*

Free-Fall Into God

To know God you must forget all you know about God. To have a personal connection with the Divine you move deep into the stillness of your consciousness. It is a place beyond religion and the constructs of the ego mind.

We dive into the bliss of the unknown to discover all that is truly real. We must go beyond the world of impermanence to discover the everlasting love and stillness of the energy that is the foundation on which the universe exists.

To enter, we peel away our outer layers of identity. The mind becomes a stilled lake from which we can see the reflection of the Divine Mind which is our true home.

Nirvana lies within and to enter God's kingdom you must leave all your concerns behind. Take off all your worries, stop trying to control the uncontrollable, and dive deep within yourself. Spirits' light will show you the way and you will bask in the splendor of your True Self which lives in atonement with God.

Journey daily into these living waters and your outer world will become as beautiful and bright as your inner being. Cleanse yourself of all that blocks the Divine light that God has placed in you. It is your job to rid yourself of your trappings and to enter with a pure and unconditioned heart.

FOR MORE INFORMATION

For more information about attending events with Manny, including his podcasts and video recordings, visit his website: www.manueljosemuros.com.

About The Author

Manuel Jose Muros (Manny) is a student of life, a metaphysical interpreter, and an avid spiritual teacher and practitioner. He had a spiritual awakening in his mid-thirties, which completely transformed his life.

An entrepreneur his entire professional life, Manny founded and served as president of three corporations. He was also the founder and vice chairman of the board of the first public Montessori Charter School in Massachusetts. He holds a BS in Pharmacology and an MBA. Manny is the owner & Spiritual Director of the Yoga Center of Newburyport and leads workshops and retreats in the US and internationally.

Manny has three grown sons. He lives in historical Newburyport, MA with his partner, Alise Ashby, an accomplished composer, songwriter, producer, and pianist.

www.ingramcontent.com/pod-product-compliance
Lightning Source LLC
Chambersburg PA
CBHW020357080526
44584CB00014B/1062